T0321286

Lead With AI

Lead With AI

Igniting Company Growth With Artificial Intelligence

Amir Elkabir

BUSINESS EXPERT PRESS

Leader in applied, concise business books

Lead With AI: Igniting Company Growth With Artificial Intelligence

Copyright © Business Expert Press, LLC, 2024

Cover design by Zeljka Kojic

Interior design by Exeter Premedia Services Private Ltd., Chennai, India

All rights reserved. No part of this publication may be reproduced, stored in a retrieval system, or transmitted in any form or by any means—electronic, mechanical, photocopy, recording, or any other except for brief quotations, not to exceed 400 words, without the prior permission of the publisher.

First published in 2024 by
Business Expert Press, LLC
222 East 46th Street, New York, NY 10017
www.businessexpertpress.com

ISBN-13: 978-1-63742-589-3 (paperback)
ISBN-13: 978-1-63742-590-9 (e-book)
ISBN-13: 978-1-63742-593-0 (hardcover)

Business Expert Press Collaborative Intelligence Collection

First edition: 2024

10 9 8 7 6 5 4 3 2 1

Dedicated to anyone with a dream of a boundless future.

Description

Forget the hype, the tech buzzwords, and the mystifying charm of AI. If you're not channeling AI for business success, it's all just noise. Whether you are aiming to pioneer technological change, fuel growth through AI, or spark its transformative power, *Lead With AI* is your blueprint.

The author—a seasoned technologist and MIT graduate—takes us on a journey to the epicenter of modern technological evolution. From the bustling innovation hub of Kendall Square to intimate study sessions unveiling pivotal AI concepts, the book goes beyond AI's technicalities to spotlight its applications in real-world business scenarios.

In a sea of AI content, *Lead With AI* stands apart. It's not just about building AI systems; it's about crafting an environment where AI truly thrives, delivering unmatched value.

How the Reader Will Benefit

This book transforms AI from a buzzword into a practical tool for industry leaders. By mastering the insights in this book, leaders, managers, and professionals will be able to:

- Integrate AI seamlessly into strategic decision making
- Recognize AI-driven opportunities throughout the company
- Assess AI's potential pitfalls and limitations in business settings
- Boost organizational performance with AI-driven strategies

Keywords

artificial intelligence; ai leadership; business transformation; machine learning; technological innovation; AI strategy; data-driven decision making; tech entrepreneurships; AI in business operations; digital transformation; leadership in the tech era; AI ethics in business; AI-driven business models; technology management; future of work; AI startups; tech consultancy; AI integration strategies; organizational change; AI solutions in business

Contents

Preface

Just last year, I found myself walking through the famous halls of MIT. This place, soaked with ideas and exploding with brainpower, was my creative happy place when it came to writing this book. But let's clear one thing up, I didn't land here because of some well-thought-out grand plan. As much as I would like to think I did that, it was more like a mid-life crisis, turbo-charged by two years of living through a pandemic.

Picture my situation—isolation, a bunch of deep thoughts, and too much time on my hands. With this self-destructive cocktail, it's no wonder my life's path got flipped upside down.

Nonetheless, I decided not to wallow. I thought, "Why not use this mess to reinvent myself?" Remembering Stephen Covey's advice to *sharpen the saw* from *The 7 Habits of Highly Effective People*, which had influenced me deeply since I read it. That was the inspiration I needed. I pressed pause on my bustling career and took a year-long break—a mix of an intellectual journey, a spiritual recharge, and quality time with my family.

My aim was to dive right back into the electrifying world of tech innovation. And where better to do that than Kendall Square, a hotspot for tech and biotech folks? Picture the tech scene as the Roman Empire; Kendall Square would be Rome at its prime. After 20 years in tech, I was ready to jump in and get my hands dirty.

Trying to understand this scene was like riding a rollercoaster in overdrive. It felt like I was lost in a sea of fancy words and complex ideas—Web 3.0, Blockchain, Crypto Assets, Metaverse, AI, Quantum Computing, Sustainability—you name it. Even seasoned investors seemed like they were just treading water, trying to keep up.

In the middle of all this, Mark Zuckerberg shook things up by turning Facebook into Meta and taking a leap into the Metaverse. However, the tech world didn't miss a beat. With the *Year of Efficiency* on the horizon, there were layoffs left and right and a sudden swerve toward AI. That's when I first heard about GPT. My buddy Andy introduced me to ChatGPT during a study group meeting one day at MIT—it seemed like a small thing, but boy, did it leave a mark. In less than five days, more than a million users had joined the service, and a couple of weeks later, I was at in a conference hosted at MIT with Sam Altman and Lex Fridman discussing the way AI was shaping the future right before my eyes.

Meanwhile, cryptocurrency, once the darling of the tech world, was having a tough time. FTX, a big exchange handling about U.S.$1 billion of transactions a day, went belly up. And the fall of Silicon Valley Bank just added to the panic.

This wild ride reshaped my view of things. I swapped my tech-heavy talk for a more down-to-earth, business-centric way of speaking. It was like learning a new language, or even picking up a musical instrument for the first time.

With the digital world evolving at lightning speed, I saw business leaders trying their best to keep up. Everyone was talking about AI, but few really got what it was about or how it could be used. And, honestly, who could blame them? AI was changing so fast it was enough to make your head spin.

On the other side, researchers were busy perfecting complicated models and working with piles of data. Ask them about it, and you'd get a vague *Black Box* answer, as if their work was some big mystery.

But in this confusion, I saw an opening. My unique mix of skills could serve as a bridge between the complicated world of tech and the practical world of business. It was a big challenge—diving deep into the murky world of AI, figuring it out, and then putting it in simple business terms.

It was a scary challenge, but the potential was huge. My goal was not just to understand AI but also to find practical ways of applying this fascinating technology, crack the code of how to methodologically spot business opportunities for AI-driven concepts, and share this knowledge as widely as I could. This book is my attempt to clear up the mystery of AI, shed some light on it, and share this knowledge with anyone who's interested.

Why Me? Why Now?

I'm not someone tucked away in a lab but more of a hands-on type of person. I've got a deep respect for academia, and I regularly find myself sliding into learner mode, because I've got a thirst for knowledge. But there's something about building and creating things that stirs up even more excitement in me. I'm someone who lives and breathes technology; I've been curious about math, science, and physics from the get-go. But it's not just about the technology for me; it's about how we can use that technology in the real world.

Looking back at my career, it's been quite an eclectic narrative. Not that I planned it that way, but as Steve Jobs said in his famous Stanford University commencement speech, "You can't connect the dots looking forward; you can only connect them looking backwards." That seems to ring true for me. I can clearly connect all the dots in my career now, but only now I'm looking in the rearview mirror.

This variety of experiences has given me a unique view of different industries, business environments, and regions around the world. I've worked in technical and managerial positions in the semiconductor industry. I've found myself lying on the floor of clean room fabs at Intel and Samsung while I was at Applied Materials. I've deployed Fintech core systems and worked with demanding clients in the high-pressure environment of banks like HSBC, Citibank, and OCBC, when I was with companies like D+H and Finastra. I've taken leading roles in the digital streaming revolution, developing and launching video streaming products to millions of households during my time at AT&T. I've even worked in the heart of Startup Nation at the most active venture capital firm in the Middle East.

But there's more to my story than the *professional experience* since engineering school. In my 20s, I was an entrepreneur running my own pub-restaurant. I've worked on a couple of cruise ships in the Mediterranean. I've been a bartender, a gas station worker, a high-school physics teacher, a military soldier for three years, and so much more.

All the examples, the business contexts, the different views, and applications you'll read about in this book come from this journey I've been on. It wasn't until I found a technology that I knew would impact every one of us, everywhere, that I realized how all these experiences came together. I'm excited to share what I've learned and how it all connects to AI.

You'll find the language in this book easy-going and approachable. That's how I am. There is no jargon that you need a dictionary for, no complex calculations, and no fancy words just for the sake of it. I choose books the same way I choose restaurants: for quality content in a relaxed, easy-going environment. That's what I hope to give you in this book.

Why Read This Book?

Many businesses are asking how we can make AI consumer capabilities, enterprise ready.

We're all in a world that's changing nonstop, where tech breakthroughs are constantly transforming the scenery. And among all these changes, one big game-changer stands out—artificial intelligence (AI). It's not just a system for making businesses run more smoothly; it's also a whole new way to understand, interact with, and shape our world.

The phrase *game-changing* only just starts to describe the huge shift AI has initiated in businesses of all sizes and sectors. AI, and the evolving field of machine learning, have moved from being just buzzwords to essential tools for any business leader who's thinking ahead. They've become priceless, doing all sorts of jobs, from speeding up product development to finetuning marketing investments. They're now key parts of how modern businesses work.

AI has become so widespread that understanding it is now a must-have, not a nice-to-have, for anyone who's making decisions in the business world. You just can't ignore AI and what it means anymore. In a world where every business decision can have big effects on a company's finances, getting AI isn't a choice—it's a must.

But, the power of AI extends beyond company boardrooms. This groundbreaking tech is set to massively change our careers, reshape our jobs, and totally revolutionize what work is. If we don't get a good handle on this changing landscape, we could make bad decisions, with serious consequences. Keeping up with AI developments isn't just about keeping up with the competition—it's about seeing changes coming and setting ourselves up for success in an AI-filled future.

Whether you're just getting started with AI, need a refresher, or work side-by-side with AI specialists, this book's goal is to give you a basic understanding of AI. It's here to give you the ability to use AI effectively to boost your work. Each chapter gives you practical knowledge, in plain language, with insights you can use in your business right away.

Among all the AI resources out there, some of which can be a bit too much, this book sets itself apart with its unique approach. While there are loads of guides to polishing your AI engineering skills, this book promises something more. It aims to help you not only build efficient AI systems but also create an environment where AI can truly thrive and give maximum value.

The main goal of this book is to make AI accessible to everyone and to make sure its benefits aren't just for those who know technical jargon. Leaders, managers, marketers, and professionals from all industries are not just watching this AI revolution; they're also key players who can shape the direction and impact of AI. By understanding what AI can and can't do and seeing opportunities for AI in an organization, you can play a key role in shaping an AI-driven future.

So, if you're ready to unleash the power of AI, change the way your business works, and make your career future-proof, let this book be your guide. Think of it as your first step on the journey to tap into the endless potential AI has to offer.

Introduction

It always starts from human intervention with only a sprinkle of AI.

My Personal Touch

As a child growing up in a quiet, northern Israeli town bordering Lebanon, my father was a significant influence on me. Every day, he would set out for a short, five-minute walk from our home to the nearby street corner. He would carry a briefcase, which he fondly referred to as the *James Bond* suitcase. At exactly 7:30 AM, he would board his daily bus to work, a routine he had established after our three-year stay in Austin, Texas, where he pursued his PhD at the University of Texas. Like clockwork, he would disembark from the same bus at the same corner at 5:15 PM. His work realm was devoid of the complexities of modern technology—no laptop, no mobile phone, no messaging platform. This was all occurred during the 1990s, when our house, which was equipped with a single phone, was free of work-related calls. His *James Bond* briefcase was filled with physical documents. Within these boundaries, my father built a distinguished career, contributing to product creation and widget manufacturing—he did it all, strictly within the limits of a typical workday.

In my 20s, I found myself working for Applied Materials. I now had a laptop and a no-frills Nokia mobile phone that was just a device for making and receiving calls. E-mails, messaging, and apps didn't exist. Fresh out of engineering school at the university, I took on the role of managing a small engineering team. Our laptops were our lifelines, and I vividly recall how my IBM ThinkPad would notify me of a new e-mail every few minutes. That sound filled me with a sense of significance, a feeling of connection. However, I often wondered—were we genuinely accomplishing more than my father had done 15 years earlier? We created products, we manufactured widgets, but could we honestly say we were more efficient than his generation?

As my career progressed, so did technology. My Nokia was eventually replaced with a Blackberry, which was soon replaced with an iPhone 3. The era of social media arrived with Facebook and instant messaging through WhatsApp. Today, my digital presence is vast. I can be reached by e-mail, accessible through either of my two laptops, or any of my three e-mail accounts. You can text me, call me, video chat, leave me a voicemail, even check if I've read your message or not. But a recurring question persists—have these advances increased my efficiency, reduced it, or kept it at the same level as before? How do I compare to my father, who managed to achieve so much with so little technology?

This perspective makes me reevaluate the role of technology in my life. As I delve deeper into the age of artificial intelligence (AI), these questions become more relevant. This transformation of work and communication through technology is a double-edged sword—it has ushered in new possibilities, but it also makes me wonder if it has made me more effective at what I do.

Often, I catch myself just watching my kids, my lively nine-year-old, Daniel, and my spirited teenager, Carmel, who's already 13. I can't help but wonder about the future they're stepping into. The stuff they're learning in school right now could be seen as old news by the time they're heading off to college. And who can say if the careers they pick will even exist when they're tossing their graduation caps into the air? It's as if I'm standing on quicksand, writing a book about AI, knowing that in 10 years or so, the world as we know it might be totally different. So, the big question is—while AI is great at helping us get more done on a small scale, can it truly change the game when we look at the bigger picture?

To me, the answer depends on a couple of things—what we're hoping AI will do for us and how we decide to guide its growth. It's crucial to add a human touch to AI before it turns us into machines. We've got to remember that we're flesh and blood, not metal and wires. Technology is racing ahead at breakneck speed, but are we? We're still designed to take things slower. We need our six to eight hours of sleep every night. We crave chit-chats and connections with others. Not too long ago, I watched an amazing TED talk by a Harvard professor who showed how keeping close social connections throughout our lives is the top thing that helps keep us happy and live longer. We still crave life's simple joys—the magic of a bedtime story, the beauty of a sunset, the happiness of a lazy day doing nothing. It's still important that we wake up and say good morning to our loved ones next to us before checking our e-mails, and it always will be. We're not robots. We're complex creatures full of feelings, not a tangle of wires and circuits.

That's not to say AI doesn't have a lot to offer. It certainly does. It can take boring, repetitive tasks off our plates, help us make better decisions by predicting outcomes, and finetune our preferences so that we can cut through all the noise and find what really matters to us. But there's a danger in falling too hard for technology and letting it distract us from the things that truly make us human.

Figuring out the balance between technology and our human lives, between AI and our own natural rhythms: it's like a dance we're all still learning. It's a bit of a juggling act, but it's one we have to do. Adopting AI doesn't mean we should let it take over. It's a tool, a really powerful one, but it's here to help us, not boss us around.

As we stride into an AI-filled future, we've got to make sure we're the ones calling the shots, not the other way around. We need to bring our humanity into our tech, to remember the importance of our natural human rhythms, and to make sure that while we're building a future with AI, we're not forgetting to live.

Back when I was a teenager, if I wanted to chat with a friend, I'd just dial their number, from memory. I kid you not, I had about 40 phone numbers memorized—friends, family, and important contacts. But then came mobile phones, and all those memorized numbers started to slip away.

I have another strong memory from when I was 25. With my girlfriend at the time, who's now my amazing wife Einat, I took a trip to Barcelona. We decided to rent a car, and I borrowed a map from the rental company. I actually memorized our whole route—the turns, street names, how far apart each turn was—everything. Now, I just tap a few buttons on my smartphone, and Google Maps or Waze lead the way. It's like my natural sense of direction has gone to sleep, thanks to technology.

This shift in our world is real, and it makes me wonder about the future my kids are stepping into. Will they know how to spell words right without relying on Grammarly, which watches their every keystroke?

Will they get to experience the thrill of hunting for and finding information themselves, or will they totally depend on AI and search engines? I'm not even going to mention dictionaries and encyclopedias. Even online resources like Wikipedia might soon be history.

As we build AI, and I'm included in that, we need to do it thoughtfully and with a strong sense of responsibility. When we talk to natural language processing systems and big language models, we should remember to use *please* and *thank you*, because these AI models learn from us. They're like children growing up in our digital world, and we want to teach them to be polite and kind. We need to make sure we don't misuse AI, taking advantage of its current inability to track the origins of data in the huge sea of information. We can't let biases creep into our AI systems and cause harm to certain groups just because the checks and balances are still trying to catch up. Right now, you're the responsible one, and so am I; we all are. We're the grownups in this somewhat chaotic scene that hasn't figured out how to govern itself because, as I mentioned earlier, tech is outpacing us. But that doesn't mean it needs to take control away from us.

We owe it to ourselves, our kids, and the generations to come to build responsible, fair, and ethical AI. The question we should be asking ourselves isn't just about what kind of AI we want, but what we need to do to build that AI. It's not just about making fancy tech, but about shaping a world that respects our humanity, a world where AI assists us, but doesn't define us. We need to weave this understanding into every part of AI development, to make sure that the world we pass onto our kids is a world they can navigate safely, ethically, and confidently.

Jumping Head First

And If I Won't Lead With AI?

Have you ever noticed that we all have distinct habits: little quirks that define our personalities and set us apart? One of mine that you might find intriguing involves reading the quotes or slogans that people choose to include in their e-mail signatures. These often range from safety admonitions such as "Don't Text And Drive" to environmental pleas like "Save Trees, Save Our Planet," along with a myriad of other thoughtful messages.

During my time at AT&T, I noticed an e-mail signature from a colleague from the Chicago office that really stood out to me. It read, "If you don't like change, you'll hate irrelevance even more." Initially, it elicited a chuckle, but on deeper reflection, it seemed almost profound. I found it insightful and, most importantly, universally applicable—it's timeless wisdom for the digital age.

You see, as human beings, we have a natural aversion to change. It's a common trait among us all. Change pushes us out of our familiar comfort zones, making us exert energy on learning and adapting to new things. We invest substantial time and effort mastering a particular domain, hoping to sit back and enjoy the ride once we've reached a certain level of proficiency. But, as life would have it, a new trend emerges or a fresh-faced boss with innovative ideas takes control, and we're forced back into learning mode. It's a cycle that many of us don't enjoy—but that's only part of the story.

On the other side of the coin, as humans, we crave relevance and a sense of purpose in what we do. That craving often supersedes our need for comfort. We want our contributions to matter, for our work to have significance. That's a feeling we value highly—sometimes even more than staying within the cozy feeling of familiarity and ease.

I will never forget a thought-provoking lecture delivered by the esteemed Professor Roberto Rigobon during my studies at MIT. I can't quote him accurately, but the crux of his theory regarding this topic is etched in my memory. He painted a picture of a life trajectory that was typical in the times of our parents and grandparents. By and large, our lives were patterned similarly across generations: We were born, we grew into children, we attended school, acquired a professional skill set or learned a craft, then we joined the workforce, and finally, we retired. This cycle, this system of life, was quite linear and straightforward.

During an era when the average lifespan was around 65 years, the pattern looked something like this: Spend six years transitioning from infancy to childhood, another decade in formal education, five years acquiring a professional skill, then work for three decades, and finally enjoy a lengthy retirement lasting around 14 years. This model worked well in a slower-paced world, with localized workplaces and minimal technological disruptions. It was entirely reasonable to take care of grandchildren or embark on the trip around the world we'd always dreamed about at 51. It did not have to be at 41.

However, the times have changed significantly, and the future holds an entirely different reality for us and our children. Two dominant forces are exerting immense pressure on our generation, challenging the conventional life strategy our parents and grandparents adhered to. The first is increased longevity—we're now living to an average of 85 years. The second, and equally disruptive, is the rapidly evolving digital world powered by groundbreaking technologies such as AI, which penetrates every aspect of our work and personal lives.

In the current era, we might spend six formative years growing from a baby to a child, followed by 12 years in school, and then about a decade more honing our professional skills, which typically includes an undergraduate degree, a graduate degree, and hands-on experience through an internship. If we plan to retire at 70, that leaves a significant four-decade-long stretch to work.

This modern timeline presents two substantial challenges. Firstly, assuming caretaking responsibilities for our grandchildren or fulfilling our lifelong travel dreams at 70 is considerably more difficult. Secondly, and more critically, given today's rapidly-paced industrial and technological advancements, can we confidently assume that what we learn in university will remain relevant and valuable four decades later?

These changes lead me to my core argument—the absolute necessity of learning to lead with AI. AI is permeating every aspect of our lives at an accelerated pace. It's crucial for people of my generation, and those who came before and will come after, to grasp at least the fundamental principles behind AI, to stay relevant and continuously contribute value in the contemporary workplace. And when I say this, I'm not just referring to programmers or software engineers. It also applies to business leaders and enterprise managers, who risk letting the world pass them by if they fail to comprehend AI and feel comfortable navigating their business objectives with it at the forefront of their strategy.

Making Sense of AI

AI is more than just a cool word we hear a lot these days. It's a powerful tool changing our world, appearing more and more in the news, powering things like chatbots, and shaking up different industries. But there's more to AI than what we first see; to truly understand it, we need to look beyond the initial excitement. This book aims to simplify AI—explaining what it does, showing its deep connection with society, and highlighting how it affects our daily lives.

Everywhere we look, we hear about the amazing things AI is doing. It's changing everything from health care to art, making our security systems better, and even guiding our daily Internet searches. With all this information, it can feel like trying to navigate a complicated maze.

In the financial services industry, AI is now taking center stage. Firstly, financial institutions are using AI to better serve their customers, enhancing solutions for everyone from the customer-facing front office to the operational back office. Secondly, they're leveraging AI to strengthen their position in the market, ensuring they remain ahead of their competitors. Thirdly, there's the allure of cost-efficiency. AI offers the potential to streamline operations and reduce costs, making it an attractive proposition for any business.

AI-driven applications are becoming increasingly popular among cloud service providers. Companies like Google and Microsoft are fervently promoting this approach. This strategy aims to initially gain a foothold and then expand their range of services. For financial institutions equipped with data know-how and technical expertise, the move toward AI goes hand in hand with a shift toward cloud services. As these entities become more entrenched in the world of AI, they're also finding more reasons to integrate cloud solutions into their daily operations.

People have different views on AI. Some see it as the start of a new era; others think it's overhyped. My goal is to help you make sense of these different opinions, giving you a balanced understanding of what AI can and can't do.

A lot of books and resources about AI get caught up in the technical details, diving deep into complex things like neural networks and math models. We'll touch on these topics too, but we're also interested in looking at how AI fits into society. We'll explore how social norms and dynamics influence AI's development, and how the growth of AI technology affects our societal structures.

People often describe AI as the *new electricity*; I want to help you understand why this comparison makes sense. Focusing only on the technical parts of AI can satisfy tech enthusiasts, but it can make us lose sight of the bigger picture. Getting too caught up in the details can make us miss out on an understanding of how AI is reshaping society. So, we aim to answer not just the techy questions, but also the bigger, philosophical ones.

This book is your partner on this journey of exploration, no matter what your experience has been with AI, computer science, or coding. Even if you already know a bit about these areas, you'll probably find some new ideas and insights. I'm not just trying to explain machine learning or statistics; but also creating a unique path through the world of AI, one that emphasizes the philosophical and societal aspects.

So why should you take the time to read this book? Maybe you're about to work with AI, or you're just curious about all the talk around this new technology. No matter why you're here, this book will give you a complete understanding of AI's role in the world; and it might even change the way you see things.

This book is more than a guide; it's an invitation to explore the multifaceted world of AI, and to wrestle with its potential, its challenges, and its deep influence on society and life as we know it. The journey might be a bit complex, but the reward is a thorough, nuanced understanding of one of today's most influential technologies.

Finding the Balance

One significant hurdle with AI and machine learning lies in striking the right balance between the technical aspects and their practical, real-world applications. While numerous resources and courses concentrate heavily on the mathematical and computing side of things, this often creates a disconnection from their practical use. My professional journey has led me to an essential realization: you don't need to comprehend every minor technical detail to make effective use of AI. The crucial thinking tool in bridging this gap is something we often utilize without even noticing—*conceptualization*.

The concept of conceptualization often comes up in basic programming and computer science classes, but its significance extends beyond just programming. Conceptualization essentially entails omitting the minutiae to concentrate on broader, more generalized concepts. In coding, we regularly employ APIs and modules without worrying about their internal workings. These components are entrusted to perform their function, allowing us to focus on what truly matters—the application we are developing. The beauty of conceptualization lies in its ability to shift our attention from being solely technology-oriented to focusing on how we can leverage that technology.

Applying conceptualization encourages us to pose the right queries and view matters from fresh perspectives. Instead of merely focusing on the functioning of a certain aspect—whether it's a machine learning algorithm or the principles of wind energy, for instance—we can delve into more effective ways of understanding these subjects. Conceptualization enables us to handle sophisticated devices without needing to understand all their nitty-gritty details. Take a wind turbine as an example—it's a network of blades, gears, and electrical systems. Despite its complexity, designers understand that users don't need to comprehend every facet of its operation. They present us with a conceptual layer, a simplified interface with easy-to-follow instructions and minimal interaction points. This conceptualization allows us to operate a complex system without getting lost in the specifics.

But conceptualization isn't limited to wind turbines and other devices. It's how we interact with everyday technology. When you use your laptop, scrolling through web pages, you might be oblivious to the sophisticated processes occurring behind the scenes. But when you click *Send* on an e-mail, you trust that it'll reach the intended recipient, even if you don't comprehend the Internet protocols making that possible. Conceptualization allows you to use these technologies without needing to grasp every technical detail.

However, it's worth noting that conceptualization isn't flawless. It inherently involves losing some detail. The more we distance ourselves from the technical elements, the more we risk compromising our ability to use them effectively. For example, if my electric scooter's battery drained and I lacked even a basic knowledge of recharging it, I'd be stranded. Hence, it's vital to develop interfaces and conceptual layers that function well and are user-friendly in their intended contexts.

In this book, we'll go deeper into the ways that conceptualization can empower leaders to grasp and harness the power of AI. We'll address practical applications, strategic considerations, and AI's societal impact. By embracing conceptualization, and honing in on its key aspects, we can navigate the sophisticated realm of AI and tap into its potential for impactful changes. Through this process, we can view AI not as an intimidating web of complexities, but as a readily accessible tool, which is capable of fostering innovation and transformation.

Becoming the Designer

I want to talk about an important job in the world of AI. It's a job that's really needed right now, but there aren't enough skilled people to fill it. We've talked about different AI uses before, but we didn't get into the nitty-gritty details like collecting data, checking systems, or planning how to roll them out. However, these things are super important. Usually, it's not the engineer's job to handle these parts. If they get stuck dealing with these issues, the project is doomed before it even starts. The goal of this book is to help you think like a designer, not like a programmer.

But as design thinkers, you'll face different challenges. Your job is to figure out the complexities of the real world and propose systems that can handle them. This complexity isn't something that can be easily automated. You need to be creative and good at problem-solving. In this book, we'll spend a lot of time identifying opportunities for AI in a structured and systematic way. Once these opportunities are found, the rest might be more of an engineering job. However, as the leader, it's your job to set the direction. It's important to understand that many failures blamed on AI are actually failures in system design and project leadership, not engineering. If a system was built according to the specs but doesn't solve the problem, it's the designer's fault for designing it wrong.

Designing an AI system is definitely a tough job, and that's exactly why we need to focus on it. It's a job that needs lots of exploration, trial and error, and the transformation of problems into doable AI tasks. As we move forward, you'll see how many sides there are to the designer's job. You're the middleman between the real world and the AI system, figuring out how information moves from one to the other and how the system's outputs are used.

What Is AI?

As AI becomes advanced there is a great advantage of
being a generalist as opposed to being a specialist.

A Dance Between Human and Machine

Getting to know artificial intelligence (AI) is like going on a thrilling journey—one that checks out what AI can do with ease, what still gets it tangled up, and how these abilities stack up against our own incredible human skills. Imagine it as a winding path of evolution, along which we'll follow AI's transformation up to today. This journey will set us up for the deep talks in the chapters to come.

At its heart, AI is an idea dreamed up by a forward-thinking pioneer, John McCarthy. He pictured it as the art and science of making smart machines, especially clever computer programs. It's all about using computers to understand and maybe even copy human smarts. But it's crucial to remember that AI isn't trying to exactly copy how the human brain works.

In the early days of AI and machine learning, there was a lot of interest in building systems based on the human brain. The idea was simple; if you could copy a load of brain neurons, you might be able to make intelligence. While modern machine learning techniques might take some ideas from this, the modern AI field isn't trying to make a perfect clone of the human brain.

So, how can we understand AI? And how did we get to where we are now? To answer these questions, let's take a quick trip down memory lane in AI's history.

The phrase *artificial intelligence* came about in the summer of 1956. Around that time, a plan was hatched to bring 10 top researchers together for a summer brainstorm at Dartmouth College in Hanover, New Hampshire. The lead organizer was John McCarthy, who had the bold goal of tackling tricky topics like language and abstraction, problem-solving, and self-improvement in just a few months. The aim of teaching computers to think like humans, driven by the hope of huge potential benefits, was a massive task. But the group was full of hope. Claude Shannon of Bell Telephone Laboratories was another pivotal figure in that research collective. We will get to his substantial contributions to the field of generative AI later in this book.

You might be wondering why they were so confident. Why did they think they could achieve such an amazing thing in the summer of 1956? The answer lies in the spirit of the time. The mid-1950s was when computers started showing serious talent in chess—a game traditionally seen as a test of intelligence. The thinking was simple: If smart people are good at chess, and computers could nail this game, then it wasn't a big jump to think that computers could be taught to be intelligent.

But does being a champ at chess really mean you're intelligent? Back then, the usual plan for computer chess was to predict 15 to 20 moves ahead and pick the move that would result in the best board position. This plan mirrors the way that top chess players play, showing a key way to develop intelligence: watch human behavior, figure out the rules and decision-making processes behind these actions, and then program these rules into a machine. When computers started winning at chess—a game seen as complicated—it sparked the belief that AI could handle many tasks that humans find less challenging.

However, as the story of AI continues, we're finding that reality can often surprise us, diverging from our assumptions. We'll dig deeper into this fascinating journey in the coming chapters. For now, think of AI as a flexible and powerful tool that isn't tied down by human biology or behavior. This broader view will give you a solid base to really appreciate AI's enormous potential, preparing you for the deep explorations to come.

Poker and Logos

Let's look at a comparison, using a poker game and routine marketing tasks as our backdrop. At first glance, many regular marketing tasks may seem less complex than a game of poker. If AI can grasp the nuanced strategies and countless possibilities of poker, couldn't it manage other tasks, potentially simpler ones, with equal efficiency? Consider the task of recognizing a company's logo. For us, a swift look at a logo is usually enough. Hence, it's reasonable to assume that a computer program would be exceptionally proficient at recognizing logos, a task we instinctively find less challenging than poker.

With that initial thought process in mind, earlier in our century, there was an attempt to develop an app that can identify if a symbol in a photo is a logo, but many predicted that this app would take a team of developers half a decade to devise. Surprisingly, this prediction was spot on; it took roughly five years for AI to reliably recognize logos. However, it's critical to underscore that this accomplishment took over 50 years from when the idea was initially proposed. A project initially planned for the summer of which McCarthy and friends came together ended up spanning more than five decades. So, why was this seemingly simple task so challenging?

Poker, despite its intricacy, conforms to well-defined rules. We can dissect the game, comprehend its rules, and translate these rules into algorithmic solutions. The initial approach to the logo recognition task adopted this logic. The theory was that logo recognition could be split into smaller problems, each solvable independently. And all that was left to be done was to identify the circle, the triangles, the lines, and voila—you've got a logo identifier!

Regrettably, reality didn't align with this hypothesis. The world doesn't operate on neatly arranged rules, and AI demanded a novel approach. As humans, we do use rules to perform tasks. For example, when identifying a logo, we might subconsciously recognize its parts and combine them to form a complete image. Early AI strategies hypothesized that if we could explicitly outline these rules, we could instruct machines to do the same. This rule-based approach had done wonders with poker, so why not apply it elsewhere? Why couldn't we simply document the rules we subconsciously follow?

The problem is that life is filled with subtleties and variations. The same logo can appear vastly different from various angles or distances. The process of building AI and machine learning models has left us astounded by the exceptional capabilities of the human brain. Tasks we execute effortlessly turn out to be monumental challenges when you try to replicate them in AI.

Take the task of handwriting recognition, a seemingly straightforward job, which is vital for tasks like sorting documents in a business setting. Given an image of handwriting, how would you formulate rules to correctly identify it? You might rely on various strategies, like identifying distinctive handwriting patterns or measuring the angles of certain strokes. Yet, when tested, these rule-based strategies performed inadequately on publicly available datasets. Once more, the task of formulating rules proved to be a daunting mountain to climb.

These repeated failures led to periods known as *AI winters* in the 1970s and 1980s. Interest dwindled, funding dried up, and progress seemed to stall. Rule-based AI appeared to be an unsolved riddle. But over 50 years later, we've made leaps in areas like vision and transaction analysis. So, how did we orchestrate this turnaround?

The answer lies in the techniques we developed in response to the shortcomings of rule-based systems. We had to reassess our understanding of intelligence. While tasks like playing poker seemed formidable for humans and logo recognition a breeze, the situation was reversed for machines. This role reversal pushes us to rethink our concept of intelligence and our definition of what it means to be *smart*.

Historically, machines functioned in ways that were based on rules. We provided clear instructions, and the machine adhered to them meticulously. But in the face of these sophisticated problems, rules seemed insufficient. A different approach began to emerge, driven by the widespread availability of data. When we realized that we couldn't effectively document the rules, we turned to data. As we continued to generate massive volumes of information, perhaps the key to AI mastery in elusive tasks lay in feeding this vast ocean of data to machines.

A Fresh Take on Intelligence

As we continue to advance in AI, we've bumped into a considerable challenge. There are numerous complex AI problems where we understand the issue at hand, but converting that understanding into instructions a machine can read is another ball game. This leaves us with two potential options. We can go down the *rule-based* path, aiming to encode our knowledge into the machine, or we can take the *statistical* path, relying on data to provide insights when the rules aren't so clear-cut.

Imagine two pictures to illustrate these strategies. The first picture represents early attempts at AI, where individuals, who knew the rules, strived to translate these into a format that machines could comprehend. The second picture portrays the statistical perspective, by which humans learn from the patterns in the data.

Each approach has its merits, but they both trip up when we are facing challenges like identifying different dog breeds. We struggle to define the exact rules, and paradoxically, examining thousands of dog pictures doesn't bring any new revelations. Consequently, neither method delivers exactly what we need.

This dilemma leads us to the heart of contemporary machine learning. Imagine rearranging these two pictures to depict a new process. Humans take a step back, and data are directly utilized to formulate the rules, without the need for human-derived insights. This transformation encapsulates the essence of current machine learning.

Initially, it might seem sensible to combine the rule-based and statistical approaches. You might believe that we could use rules to extract insights from the data, which in turn would broaden our understanding and help us to formulate better rules. However, this process only emphasizes the redundancy of human involvement. Our role as intermediaries doesn't contribute anything substantial. In fact, the most effective learning occurs when we remove ourselves from the process entirely. We allow the insights derived from the data to directly shape the rules, without human intervention. We become observers of the process, reaping its benefits. This new approach demonstrates the true power of data-driven rule formation, the cornerstone of modern machine learning.

The Algorithmic and Data Modeling Divide

In the world of data science, there are two main cultures: algorithmic modeling and data modeling. Understanding the difference will help you see why we're moving from simply understanding data to using algorithms to make predictions.

Imagine traditional statistical modeling as a process where you start with some raw data—let's call it *X*. These data are then transformed by business operations, market dynamics, or economic factors, leading to a result we can see. For a long time, the goal has been to predict this result, analyzing how different pieces fit together, and making sure the model makes sense. It's a bit like trying to put together a puzzle, where the picture is made up of the variables influencing the result.

However, some of the early innovators in statistics and machine learning weren't happy with this traditional approach. They felt it wasn't up to the task of solving the many predictive problems we face today. They suggested a major shift to a more flexible approach that puts data front and center. This new approach cares more about making accurate predictions than understanding every detail of how the data are connected.

Let's think about some real-life situations: predicting stock prices based on economic indicators guessing customer behavior from purchase history, figuring out if an e-mail will be marked as spam based on its content, or even predicting if a product will succeed from its launch strategy. Even though these questions are different, they all boil down to the same thing—using inputs to predict outputs. This is the core idea behind predictive modeling; no matter what the inputs are or how they change, we can still make accurate predictions about what will happen next.

This principle of predictive modeling is like a Swiss army knife. It can be applied in various contexts, proving just how important machine learning is in today's predictive analysis.

On the one hand, we have the data modeling culture. It's like being a detective, always trying to understand the causal mechanisms and underlying models of the business world. It's about wanting to know what happens inside the *black box* of transformations from input to output. It's all about the details and understanding the inner workings of the system.

On the other hand, the algorithmic modeling culture, the heart of modern AI, doesn't lose sleep over what happens inside this *black box*. Its main job is to make accurate predictions, without worrying too much about the rules involved. This culture is about approximating the world's existing rules, with less concern for understanding or being exact about these rules. It's like aiming for the finish line without caring too much about the journey.

Now, this might seem a bit frustrating, especially because it doesn't pay much attention to the causal relationships within data. But its main goal is clear—making predictions we can count on.

This approach might not sit well with everyone, but it represents a practical, results-oriented mindset that matches the pace of today's industries. It supports the idea that utility is more important than full understanding and that making accurate predictions is more valuable than explaining everything. At the end of the day, what matters most is not how we got the results, but the results themselves. And, in our data-driven world, the ability to make accurate predictions is becoming more and more valuable.

Algorithmic Versus Data Modeling

Let's dive deeper into how algorithmic and data modeling cultures differ by looking at a different example. Let's say we're trying to predict sales for a retail business. Here's the $1 million question: Do we need to fully understand all the nuances of consumer behavior, or is it enough to just make accurate predictions? If we can skip the understanding part and go straight to predicting sales accurately, wouldn't that be really useful? This is what the algorithmic modeling culture is all about—it's also the foundation of machine learning.

But don't forget, there's definitely still room for the data modeling approach, especially when we're aiming not just to make accurate predictions but also to build a comprehensive model of the business world. Let's say we're trying to understand the impact of different marketing strategies on sales. We might want to investigate the actual impact of strategies like price reductions or ad campaigns. These scenarios need more than just predictions; they require an understanding of cause and effect—the key to understanding any business decision. In such cases, data modeling, with its focus on understanding and clarity, might come out on top.

However, machine learning isn't some magical solution. It can make simple mistakes because it doesn't possess the natural understanding that humans do. A machine learning model can make predictions based on patterns it detects from the data, but it doesn't always get the *why* behind those patterns. It's like a parrot that can mimic words but doesn't understand what they mean.

The real power of machine learning comes from its procedural and algorithmic nature. It has an impressive ability to predict outputs from inputs without needing to understand what happens in the middle. This makes it a powerful tool for a bunch of tasks where the main goal isn't necessarily to understand the whole process but to accurately predict the results.

As we watch the progress of AI, the contrast between algorithmic modeling and data modeling gets more and more intriguing. Both cultures, each with their unique strengths and weaknesses, offer different ways to use data to understand and predict the world of business. The best strategy might not be to choose one over the other but to blend the strengths of both cultures. By doing this, we might be able to build powerful, predictive models that not only give accurate predictions but also give us deep insights into our business world.

Cracking the Code in a Data-Dominated World

Data science is an exciting field, and it's full of surprising turns. Take Netflix's recommendation algorithm as an example. Instead of sticking to human-made rules, it creates its own rules directly from the data. Machine learning does the rule-making, and then we can go back and look at these rules to see if we can learn something new. But as these rules become increasingly complex and numerous, our ability to check each one starts to decline.

Fast forward to 2023, and some of our most crucial models have become so sophisticated that it's not feasible to fully examine them. But this doesn't mean these models are outdated or worthless. It's quite the opposite. Despite their complexity, these models are still vital tools in our data-centric world. The answer isn't to toss them aside because they're tough to comprehend, but to adjust our approach to handling them.

When we try to avoid unexpected problems that could cause harm, ensuring safety becomes our top priority. Let's think about customer product review analysis as an example. Even though we can't entirely comprehend the process, we can still examine the data and get a sense of which words are associated with positive or negative reviews. Occasionally, we might stumble upon surprises, like the term *sick*, which in some contexts, can have positive connotations.

These unexpected outcomes show that our understanding of language and its nuances is far from perfect. For instance, we might not have initially thought of emojis as a helpful predictor in customer review analysis. But upon examining the data, it's clear that emojis hold a lot of predictive power. Similarly, when we're trying to tell different customers apart, specific phrases and language styles can significantly impact our predictions. This reminds us that our understanding of language and our ability to set rules might not be as complete as we believe.

This raises an intriguing question: Do we need to understand what's happening behind the scenes? In some scenarios, the answer might be no. But there might be situations where understanding the underlying process is vital for drawing meaningful conclusions or making trustworthy predictions.

A crucial lesson we can take from these observations is that language analysis, like customer review analysis, can be treated like any other data. We can apply this approach to any language, even those we're unfamiliar with, without needing to understand the language itself. It's like the way an intelligent alien might analyze our languages: They wouldn't have any preconceived notions about it but would nonetheless be able to detect patterns and rules.

But that doesn't mean all rules are irrelevant. Some areas, like algorithmic trading, still heavily rely on well-established rules. So, it's vital to understand the difference between what we call *open-world* problems, where the rules are unclear or hard to nail down, and *closed-world* problems, where the rules are known and straightforward. Open-world problems include areas like finance, social media trends, climate change, certain aspects of physics, and sensor data. Closed-world problems are more about well-defined and controlled environments.

In the constantly evolving world of AI, both algorithmic and data modeling continue to advance and shape our understanding. Both have their strengths and weaknesses, but together, they provide a comprehensive picture of the world and our role in it. As we continue exploring these two cultures, the fascinating interplay between rules, understanding, and data in intelligence keeps spinning an engaging tale. It's a narrative that's steering the course of AI and our journey toward a data-driven world.

Key Takeaways

- AI's Many Hats: AI isn't just about building machines that can think like humans. It's a varied field that's about creating systems that can boost our abilities, tackle complex problems, and make decisions on their own.
- AI's Two Pillars: AI is built on two basic principles. The first is about making rules based on our understanding of a problem and then programming these rules into a machine. The second approach, which is the main one used in modern machine learning, is about creating rules straight from the data.
- Moving to Data-Driven Models: There's been a big shift from AI based on rules to models driven by data. We're relying more and more on machine learning to find patterns and insights in huge amounts of data.
- The Role of Statistics in AI: Statistics—the study of learning from data—plays a central part in AI. It helps us understand the world and makes it possible to create data-driven rules when the ones based on human understanding just don't cut it.
- Two Sides of Statistical Modeling: Data science is divided into two camps—data modeling, which aims to understand the causes and basic models, and algorithmic modeling (or machine learning), which is all about making accurate predictions, regardless of whether we understand the process involved.
- Striking the Balance Between Predictions and Understanding: While the main goal is to make accurate predictions, there can be times when it is important to understand the causal process behind an event. The best approach might be to use the strengths of both algorithmic and data modeling.
- Open-World Versus Closed-World Problems: It's important to tell the difference between *open-world* problems, where the rules are hard to pin down or unclear, and *closed-world* problems, where the rules are clear and straightforward.

Knowing what kind of problem we're dealing with can help us figure out the best way to tackle it.

- Dealing With Complex Models: As AI models get more and more complex, the way we manage them needs to change too. Making sure everything is safe and protecting against unexpected problems become the key, even when we can't fully understand the model.

Learning Machine Learning

Success isn't about data collection, it's about data management and insight.

You've Cracked the AI Code's First Layers

Nice job! You've just taken your first steps into the world of AI, diving headfirst into its complexities, checking out potential bumps in the road, and poking around its limits. We've discovered that AI is less about brainy magic and more about the wonder of statistics. Now, as we dig deeper into this fascinating topic, let's get to know the powerhouse behind modern AI—machine learning.

Machine learning, a term that keeps popping up in AI discussions, has played a big part in shaping the AI world we see today. In this chapter, we'll boil machine learning down to its core. We'll tackle questions like:

"What exactly is machine learning?"
"How does it show up in everyday stuff?"
"What kind of problems can it help solve?"

To gain a deeper understanding of machine learning, it is helpful to compare it with something more familiar like traditional programming. You've probably used programs or apps that take some data (inputs) and spit out results (outputs). The secret sauce in these operations is a set of rules, cleverly crafted by programmers, that turn inputs into outputs.

In the world of traditional programming, these rules are key. They're carefully put together to guide the computer from inputs to the outputs you want. Like a hardworking assistant, the computer follows these instructions to the letter. If you tell it to square a number, it'll do just that, without fail, day in and day out. But the world of machine learning is a whole different ballgame.

Machine learning sets itself apart from traditional statistics by putting the spotlight on prediction instead of cause and effect. Let's say you're about to go outside, and you're wondering whether to bring an umbrella. You'd probably check the weather forecast to make a smart decision. The forecast doesn't need to explain how clouds form or how an umbrella works. And it can't change the weather. All it does is give you a prediction, helping you make a better decision.

In the same way, machine learning is great at making predictions. Think about personalized recommendations, which are basically predictions of what people will like, leading to custom-made suggestions. These recommendations might not explain why people like what they like or give ways to change their tastes. But they're a top-notch tool for predicting what people might enjoy.

Seeing this shift in focus—from understanding why to predicting what—uncovers the real power of machine learning. As we understand its limits, we can better appreciate what it can do and use its capabilities more wisely and skillfully.

Breathing Life Into Machine Learning With Music

Let's breathe some life into this concept with a completely new real-world example: Spotify, a popular online music streaming service known for its intelligent music recommendations. If you aren't familiar with Spotify, it generates personalized playlists, offering listeners a curation of songs they might enjoy. Imagine asking Spotify, "Based on my taste, what songs would I enjoy?" In seconds, you receive a playlist filled with potential new favorites—a true spectacle of machine learning magic. Now, let's peek behind the curtain and see how this all comes together.

Spotify's extensive database includes millions of songs, each with its own set of features like genre, tempo, key, and lyrics. It also considers your personal listening history and preferences. Somehow, all these data get transformed into a personalized music selection—your *Discover Weekly*. Converting raw information into a playlist might seem confusing, and you might be wondering how rules can be created to do this.

Professional DJs and music curators do this kind of music matching all the time, right? They consider various characteristics of songs and create playlists that resonate with their audience's taste. You might think they follow a fixed set of rules—pick a certain genre, match the tempo, choose the same key, and maybe sprinkle in a few surprise tracks for excitement. Sounds straightforward enough, doesn't it? Unfortunately, it's far from straightforward.

The process we're discussing—that turns inputs (song features and listener preferences) into outputs (playlists)—isn't that simple to devise. It's like a mysterious riddle box. Unlocking the secret of this box is the real challenge.

Machine Learning in Our Everyday Lives

You will be amazed at how frequently we encounter prediction problems—they're an integral part of our daily lives. Let's return to our music recommendation example. Sure, the concept of considering listener preferences (inputs) and coming up with a personalized playlist (output) seem straightforward. But in reality, it's anything but. The rules guiding these predictions can be incredibly complex and committing them to code is a challenging task. This is a common theme we've encountered throughout our exploration of AI and machine learning.

But here's the silver lining. Despite these obstacles, machine learning can take on a broad range of problems: predicting someone's preferred workout routine, determining whether a student will pass or fail a course, or forecasting shifts in fashion trends. Machine learning can handle it all. What connects these scenarios is our aim to predict an outcome (Y) based on certain inputs (X), even when the rulebook remains obscure.

The best part is that we don't have to devise these rules ourselves. We let the data do the heavy lifting and learn the rules for us. We're swamped with data these days. The tricky part is figuring out how to use these data to find these rules when it's impractical (or impossible) to write them down.

Before we dive deeper, it's crucial to understand what these data look like. With Spotify, we examined aspects like song genres, listener habits, and tempo and tried to predict music preferences. But what other historical data could be beneficial? What measurements might prove useful, and where can we find these data? These questions touch the core of the Xs and Ys in our prediction problem.

The concept of a machine learning problem might seem somewhat nebulous at this stage. But believe it or not, you've probably encountered it in your daily life. Let's circle back to the Spotify example. Imagine being handed all these data and instructed to make predictions. One of the first strategies you'd probably deploy is regression—a statistical method you may already be familiar with.

Regression, in its simplest form, means drawing a line through a cluster of data points on a graph. It might not seem like high-tech machine learning, but it's one of the foundational elements of the field, and you'll find it in any machine learning textbook. This tool allows us to make predictions based on the trend the line displays. For example, given a listener's past playlist, you could use a regression line to guess their next favorite song.

While this might sound overly simplistic, the fundamental problem that regression solves is the same one we're aiming to solve with machine learning. It's all about identifying patterns and making accurate predictions. This just goes to show that machine learning permeates our daily lives, whether we're aware of it or not.

The Gears Behind Machine Learning

Regression gives us a sneak peek into what makes machine learning tick. The journey starts with you getting some inputs (Xs) and outputs (Ys). You use regression, which draws a line, or as we call it, establishes *weights*. These are your ticket to making future predictions. This is like the mystery box we've been talking about: data go in one side, and predictions come out the other. We usually call these predictions Y-hats, to tell them apart from the real data points, or Ys.

Looking at it this way, regression is doing exactly what machine learning aims to do: give me data, and I'll hand you back this *mystery box* that can make predictions.

What's interesting is that there are two separate algorithms at work here. If the word *algorithm* feels a bit scary, think of it as just a techy word for a program that takes in inputs and spits out outputs. In this case, we've got two of these programs doing the heavy lifting.

The first is the regression algorithm itself. This is the one that knows how to take data and turn it into weights or coefficients. The second is all about these weights or coefficients. This algorithm takes the inputs, multiplies them by the weights, and adds them all up, and you've got a predicted price. These are two separate programs working together. It's important to see them as two different things. The first algorithm takes in some data and makes the rules. The second one uses these rules on inputs to make predictions.

When it comes to regression, these are two separate steps. To make it easier to understand, let's say we only have the destination of a wanted flight and we want to predict its price. What role does the regression algorithm play here? It looks at the data and thinks about the different lines it could draw. Maybe it considers one line and then another. Initially, all these lines are in the running.

This thinking process is crucial to understanding machine learning. It not only lays out the basics but also pulls back the curtain on the process. It takes machine learning from being a mystery box to being an open book that we can read, understand, and eventually use to handle all sorts of tricky prediction problems. Getting the hang of and using these two algorithms—the one that turns data into weights and the other that uses weights to make predictions—are at the heart of machine learning.

Regression and Beyond

When you strip it all down, regression is an algorithm designed to find the line that best fits the data. That's Step 1. Once this line (which we represent as weights or coefficients) is all set up, you've got a prediction tool ready to go. Let's say a new house pops up for sale. You know its square footage, and you want to guess its price. You'd use the line you've drawn to make a prediction.

So, we've got two distinct parts here:

1. The regression algorithm figures out the line (or weights or coefficients).
2. Once the weights are in place, you can make predictions about outputs based on inputs. These two parts are what regression is all about.

But remember, there's a whole bunch of ways to do regression, and the method you choose can change depending on what you need it for. A common approach is all about reducing error, but that's not the only way to do it.

It all starts to make more sense if we think of regression as a training algorithm and the weights as a model. With this new way of thinking, we've just taken a step into the broader world of machine learning.

This step means we're moving from just dealing with lines and weights to managing more complex functions and models. For example, a machine learning model might not just fit a line to the data but discover a complicated, nonlinear relationship.

In general, machine learning models can deal with more complexity than linear regression. These models could potentially be some complex function of all these inputs, letting us find and use complex patterns in the data. As the complexity gets turned up, we need more data and more advanced training algorithms.

This added complexity brings tradeoffs. While simpler models might need less data, more complex functions usually require more data. Decisions about how much data and complexity to use are typically made by AI engineers.

Moreover, while regression usually predicts continuous numbers, such as a stock price, machine learning can handle a wider range of outputs. It can work with discrete outputs, in a process known as classification, not just regression. Even though this seems like a big jump, the same machine learning framework can tackle a wide variety of problems.

In this two-algorithm view, we basically keep the same structure but add more complexity:

1. A training algorithm takes in data and comes up with a model. A lot of work goes into developing better training algorithms, and we have a good understanding of them.
2. The model makes predictions. It's a program that turns inputs into outputs. While simpler models might be easy to understand (like the coefficients in regression), more complex models often act like mystery boxes. We might not know exactly what's happening inside, but that doesn't stop us from using them effectively.

To sum it up, both regression and machine learning involve a two-step process: making a model from data and then using that model to make predictions. The main difference is in the level of complexity each method can handle. While regression is great for simple, linear relationships, machine learning is built to tackle more complex patterns and a wider range of prediction tasks.

The Art and Science in Machine Learning

We start to see that creating models is a blend of science and art. The models are molded not only by finessing the algorithms but also by adjusting the data we feed them. Let's consider an example.

Suppose we're attempting to predict a user's favorite song. What if we switched things up and tried to predict their favorite song but adjusted for their recent listening habits? Tweaking the output like this and also adjusting the inputs—such as including the user's most frequently played genre—result in a different model.

While our training algorithm remains constant, it's the data we modify that lead to a unique model. This practice of changing the model by adjusting the data it utilizes is similar to programming the system.

However, it's crucial to highlight the inflexibility in machine learning. A model that's trained on a specific set of data can't be arbitrarily applied to a different dataset. If a regression model is designed to use four variables, it can't just churn out predictions based on only three variables. This rigidity serves as a reminder that the system doesn't possess its own intelligence—it's remarkably literal, adhering to the exact structure we've established.

As the system's designer, you enjoy the liberty to make choices—which data to include, which to omit, and what outcome to predict. This flexibility allows for tweaks and adjustments based on your intuition. But, it's vital to remember the limitations. For example, if you're predicting a user's favorite song, leaving the data on their most-played artist out of your model could lead to systematic errors.

Gathering and curating the data that fuel your models can be a task in itself. In our increasingly digital world, much of what we do leaves digital trails that can be harnessed for machine learning. Streaming history, genre preferences, and online behavior all contribute to a vast pool of data that can enhance machine learning models. However, easy access to data also brings its own challenges, provoking questions about surveillance, privacy, and fair data representation.

Securing the data for your machine learning models adds another layer of complexity. Does the necessary data exist? Is it within your budget? Are there legal or privacy restrictions that prevent its use? Addressing these questions is a vital part of the multifaceted task of building a model.

Navigating the world of machine learning is similar to learning to ask the right questions. What are the inputs? What are the outputs? Where are the data sourced from? Grasping these elements is pivotal to understanding the system. Without this understanding, you won't fully comprehend how the model operates and thus won't be able to effectively tweak or troubleshoot it.

Taking a step back, we've navigated the nuances and intricacies of machine learning, from prediction problems to the art and science of model construction. Our journey has shown that, while the process may be challenging, the capability and potential of machine learning to make accurate predictions is truly revolutionary. The opportunity to experiment, the necessity for careful data curation, and the challenge of dealing with complex models make this field an exciting new frontier of innovation. It's a journey filled with wonder and discovery, with each step unveiling more about the delicate balance between data and prediction.

Key Takeaways

- Mastering Predictions: Where machine learning really shines is in its capacity to handle prediction problems. Whether it's estimating house prices or foreseeing disease outcomes, traditional programming often stumbles where machine learning strides ahead. These problems usually involve predicting an output (Y) based on given inputs (X) using a rule set crafted from learning.
- The Heart and Soul: Data are the life-giving essence that powers machine learning systems. These data, or the features used to predict outcomes, can come from varied sources and take on diverse forms, bestowing each machine learning model with its unique persona.
- Unraveling Regression: Regression, a basic part of machine learning, is a process that takes place in two phases. It first

detects a line or set of weights based on input data, and this
line or these weights are then used to predict future outcomes.

- The Two-Way Algorithm: Regression consists of two separate
  algorithms. The first forms the rules from data (the regression
  algorithm), while the second uses these rules to make
  predictions.
- Machine Learning Versus Regression: Regression and machine
  learning both follow the two-phase process of creating
  a model from data and then using this model to make
  predictions. However, machine learning outdoes regression
  when it comes to managing complex patterns and a wider
  array of prediction tasks.
- The Artistry and Precision of Model Building: Constructing
  machine learning models is a delicate interplay of art and
  science, shaped by adjusting the data we feed into the models
  and finetuning the algorithms. Bear in mind that models are
  exact and rigid, operating strictly within the precise format we
  establish.
- Vital Decisions About Data: Making the right calls about
  what data to include and exclude is crucial when building
  a model. Overlooking key features could lead to errors in
  predictions.
- Data Privacy and Ethical Queries: The abundance of digital
  data brings its own set of hurdles, including surveillance,
  privacy, and fair representation. It's vital to keep these issues at
  the forefront when collecting data.
- Grasping Inputs, Outputs, and Data Source: Understanding
  what the inputs and outputs are, and where the data originate
  from, is an essential part of comprehending the model.
  This understanding enables you to effectively tweak and
  troubleshoot the model.

Under the Hood

We are at a time where the algorithms write the code that improves the algorithm.

A Quick Refresher

Before we dig in further, let's take a moment to go over what we've covered so far. Remember when we started? We identified particular problems, a combination of inputs and outputs, and we gave them to what we called a training algorithm. This algorithm will then evolve into a model, which is a handy tool that can take on tasks like sorting or predicting. It just needs a set of inputs to make predictions. That's machine learning in a nutshell.

What's cool about this is the way it can adapt to loads of tasks that we come across in our daily life. Imagine being able to predict if someone's going to fail to pay back a loan, or if a student is likely to ace their exams, or even if a former criminal is likely to return to crime. The range of possibilities is huge and really interesting.

Yet, despite this interest, we often avoid trying to understand the ins and outs of what's *under the hood*, to figure out how it works. Our main way of controlling it tends to be the kind of data we give it—the food for the beast. Remember when we talked about how crucial it is to understand a system's inputs and outputs? If you can't nail them down accurately, you're basically sailing in the dark. The aim is to map your inputs as accurately as your tools allow.

Earlier, we also began making a cheat-sheet—a set of key questions that you should be able to answer about any system. If these questions leave you stumped, it's a warning sign that it's time to dig deeper, to understand the maze of the system's inner workings. These questions revolve around the inputs and outputs—how the outputs are made, what real-world measurements bring the system to life, and where the data comes from and how well it's been cared for.

It's worth repeating that machine learning isn't like your usual programming, where code is king. Instead, in the world of machine learning, the code, nestled in the training algorithm, is pretty much standardized. The secret to getting the system to do what you want is to show it, through examples, what you want it to do. This might seem tricky, but it often turns out to be the toughest part of working with modern machine learning systems. Training algorithms, expertly shaped by the pros, are readily available to us—stored in countless Internet libraries. The real challenge isn't finding the algorithm—it's finding the right data to solve the problem you're trying to fix.

Peeling Back the Layers With Case Studies

Let's look at the world of online shopping. Picture this: we're trying to guess what a customer might want to buy next based on what they've bought before. Sounds pretty straightforward, right? You put in the customer's past purchases, and boom, out pops a suggestion, like *ecofriendly products* or *luxury items*. But, once you start to dig into what's really going into and coming out of this system, things get a bit tricky. Ever thought about where these product recommendations come from? If you're no shopping guru, you might need to use extra information, like customer reviews or surveys, and use those results as your labels.

The accuracy of your labels really depends on how well the retailer knows their customers. If the retailer misses some hints about changing customer tastes, your model will be left in the dark. On the other hand, customer reviews might reveal trends that aren't quite so obvious. These small things can make a big difference to your results.

We'll take a closer look at these details, especially the way that labels made using human judgment stack up against labels pulled straight from the data. So far, we've been pretty chill about our labels—tagging *eco-conscious* or *luxury-lover* without really thinking about where this information comes from. But the more we get into it, the more we see the limits of different methods and how they can shape what we're able to do.

Think about farming. In places where the weather's been all over the place because of climate change, farmers have had to switch up their planting plans. One idea that came up was to predict crop yields based on weather patterns and soil conditions. How would you map out the inputs and outputs here? Where would you get the data? What exactly are you trying to guess?

Let's say you're trying to guess a farmer's crop yield. What information would you need to make this guess? Would you just use their past yields and weather records?

To build the model, you'd feed these pairs of X and Y (the weather and soil conditions and their related yields) into your training algorithm. This data, taken from databases or spreadsheets of crop records and weather reports, gets crunched by your training algorithm to spit out the model you want.

It's crucial to think about the effects of the data we use to train these models. Thinking back to the farming example, one big factor that might slip through the cracks is the farmers' access to modern farming tech. This is a big deal because it often shows differences in resources among farmers and tells us more about their farming practices. Farmers with less resources might have higher or lower yields than expected based on the tools or methods they use. Ignoring this key factor can mess up your predictions.

This goes to show that, even if we don't know the ins and outs of the model, we can still spot potential issues as long as we know what data is being used. This naturally brings us to our next big question—how should we use these predictions?

Of course, we can create a system to guess crop yields, but whether this is ethical or not depends on how we use it. If these predictions are used to interfere with market prices, it could make existing inequalities in farming even worse. But if these predictions are used to help farmers who need extra support, it could lead to more equal farming results. Therefore, how we use these predictions is a key factor in deciding whether such a system is ethical or not.

A Case of Content Moderation

Now let's turn our attention to the impact of machine learning on the rapidly growing world of social media. As the digital landscape keeps getting bigger, social media platforms are turning to machine learning to help with the huge job of managing content. Let's take a look at Facebook's journey. In the beginning, the company hired thousands of people whose main job was to manage the massive amount of content. They had to wade through endless streams of posts, marking each one as either adhering to the platform's content rules or not.

These marks, the Y in our inputs and outputs, create a treasure trove of data for a machine learning system. The X here would be the text, image, or video of the post, while the Y is a tag that tells us if the content breaks the platform's rules. This system is the foundation of most online content management processes today.

It's important to remember that when a platform boasts about using AI for content management, it's simply automating the previously human-led process of checking content. The AI or machine learning model isn't bringing anything new; it's just reflecting the data given by human reviewers, but on a much larger scale.

A key point here is understanding the crucial role the data source plays in the machine learning system. The data mainly comes from the platform itself, with human operators manually tagging each item. However, this system can cause potential problems, especially when the original human-tagged data is biased or flawed. This could lead to the machine learning model producing biased or slanted outputs, and maintaining or even increasing existing biases.

We're stuck in a cycle of collecting data, feeding it into a training algorithm to create a model, and then using that model to predict or categorize new data. This process is like a careful dance, with each step affecting the next. The effects of these steps can range from being hugely beneficial to potentially harmful, depending on how we use and interpret the outputs.

For example, imagine a situation where the human managers have a bias against a certain group. If these biases seep into the Y tags, the machine learning model, trained on this biased data, will reflect these biases when managing new content. This creates an automated system that magnifies human bias instead of reducing it.

The interconnected nature of these steps also creates chances for positive impacts. If the human management team is well trained, and the tagging process carefully designed to avoid bias and inconsistency, then the machine learning model could help create a safer and more balanced digital space. By learning from accurate and fair tags, the AI system could efficiently go through a huge amount of content and help maintain the platform's standards.

This highlights the huge importance of the source and quality of the input data, the careful design of the training algorithm, and the responsible use of the model's output. Each step in the machine learning journey comes with potential risks—but it also offers the potential for significant, beneficial contributions to social media platforms and beyond. It's a difficult dance, but it is necessary to master it.

Decision Trees and Their Practical Uses

Up until now, you might think we're pulling off some kind of trick. We feed in some inputs, out come the outputs, and our training algorithm somehow finds the patterns in between. But as we go deeper into machine learning, we'll start to uncover the magic under the hood. If you know about regression, you've got a head start in the machine learning race. But regression is just one part of the story. So, let's dive into a different type of machine learning model.

It's fine if you don't fully understand every little thing about these models right now, but there are many benefits to having a basic handle on how they work. This can satisfy your curiosity, help you make better decisions about what data to use, and even gear you up for better conversations with the tech geeks. So, with these benefits in mind, let's check out decision trees, one of the popular tools used in the machine learning arena.

Let's circle back to our example about predicting what kind of playlists Spotify users will like. First off, we need to gather some juicy data. Suppose we have an intern who pulls together information on eight users, including things like their listening history, favorite genres, and most played songs. We could use regression to create a linear equation linking these factors to the playlist preferences. But sometimes, regression isn't the best fit, especially when we think there might be some nonlinear connections between the variables.

Assuming that regression doesn't feel quite right and we're keen to try something a bit more complex, let me introduce decision trees. A decision tree, as shown in your go-to machine learning book, might look like a flowchart that asks a bunch of questions to guide you to a prediction. Let's try to make one using our Spotify data.

At first, we can create a simple tree that separates users based on their favorite genres, predicting the kind of playlists they'd like accordingly. This tree could predict a user's playlist preference based on their music genre preference. Or we could categorize users based on their most played songs, giving us a different tree. The predicted playlists for each branch are simply the most liked playlists of the users who fit those specific conditions.

But we can push it further. We can build a more complex tree by first finding out the favorite genre, and then, within each category, their most played songs. This two-layer tree can make predictions based on these two factors. Remember, all these predictions are made from averages we get from our data. Even though we're only dealing with eight users, we can create unique models that make predictions for new users.

So, what's the job of a training algorithm? Basically, the algorithm looks through all possible decision trees and picks the best one based on certain benchmarks. But what does *best* mean in the context of predicting Spotify playlists? Naturally, we want accuracy, that is, how close your predictions are to the actual playlists the users liked.

Consider three possible trees. Tree 1 has an average error rate of 10 percent, Tree 2's error rate is 30 percent, and Tree 3's error rate is 5 percent. You might think that we should pick Tree 3, as it makes the least errors.

However, in the machine learning world, we make a clear distinction between the data we use to train our models and the data we use to test them. It's crucial to understand that if we judge our model on the same data it was trained on, it might seem highly accurate. But that doesn't mean it'll do just as well on different data. This is especially true if we fit the data to a complex model, a scenario known as overfitting. Overfitting leads to predictions as reliable as a chocolate teapot.

This brings us to the idea of a balance between how fancy our model is and how much data we have. More complicated models need more data because the complexity tends to spread the data thin, making it less reliable. That's why, we prefer to keep things simple, both for intuitive and technical reasons. If our model gets too complicated, we risk learning more about the random noise in the data than the meaningful patterns in our unpredictable and noisy world.

Back to our trees, Tree 3 might have the smallest error rate, but its data is stretched thinner than Tree 1, which only errs a bit more. The best choice isn't cut and dried—it's more of a judgment call. This is where the job of a training algorithm comes in handy: it combs through the possible rules and picks the one that strikes the best balance between accuracy and simplicity. It's as much of an art as a science, and that's what makes it so interesting. If Spotify solely aimed to predict your top track, it would incessantly loop that one song, likely driving you to distraction. By design, it needs a margin of unpredictability to recognize patterns and even occasionally introduces tracks for which it lacks any prior data about your preferences.

So, there you go; decision trees aren't as mysterious as they first seem. Getting to grips with their basics and how they're built allows you to use them in your work to make predictions and guide decisions. Remember, the beauty of machine learning isn't just in the complicated models and algorithms, but also in the insights, you can pull out of your data.

The Journey Beyond Decision Trees

Up until now, our machine learning under the hood adventure has focused on decision trees. But, as you might have guessed, they're not the only tool in our toolbox. Our journey also brushes past other popular methods like regression analysis and neural networks, each dancing to the beat of its own training algorithm and offering different levels of complexity.

Think about regression analysis as being like a skilled woodworker carefully shaping a piece of wood, slowly revealing the best straight line. Or picture a neural network as a bustling city of interconnected nodes, each connection needing its own numerical code. This step-by-step, refining process is what we call gradient descent.

Despite their unique styles, all training algorithms have the same goal: to find the best model from the chosen category. So, when you're looking for a particular type of model, your training algorithm is like a treasure hunter, searching the landscape to find the best model of that type.

From experience, I can tell you what sitting in a beginners' machine learning class looks like. A lot of the class will be about defining a set of rules or a model class—like decision trees—and then using a unique training algorithm to find the perfect model. This dance between accuracy, simplicity, and complexity, all under the watchful eye of the available data, is what makes machine learning so cool.

But remember, these principles aren't going solo. They're part of a complex dance, constantly trying to balance accuracy and simplicity. The aim is to build a model strong enough to read data correctly, but not so complicated that it starts to see patterns that don't exist. Every model, whether it's based on regression, a decision tree, or a neural network, has its strengths, weaknesses, and quirks. Which model you choose depends on the problem you're trying to solve and the data you have.

The beauty of machine learning is this complex interaction of data, models, and algorithms. As we go deeper into the world of machine learning, remember that while it might seem overwhelming at times, it's this very complexity that makes it so fascinating and fun to explore.

From our journey so far, it's clear that machine learning isn't magic. It's a tool, built on solid mathematical principles, which can solve specific problems by finding patterns in data. It's a process where algorithms learn from data to make predictions or decisions, without needing a step-by-step guide. The exciting part is that, while we create the algorithms, it's the same algorithms that create the models, which then produce the predictions. It's quite a cycle, right?

With that thought, I will wrap up this chapter—not ending, just taking a break, and catching our breath in this ongoing marathon. In the following chapters, we'll dig deeper, learn more, and keep exploring many other facets of machine learning.

Key Takeaways

- Machine Learning Basics: Imagine machine learning as a super handy tool kit, helping us to see patterns in a bunch of data. This tool kit is backed up by some serious math techniques. It's like training computer programs to learn from data and make guesses or decisions without having to manually code every little step.

- Getting to Know Inputs and Outputs: In machine learning lingo, X and Y are our shorthand for inputs and outputs. The input data, or X, can be all sorts of things like words, pictures, videos … you name it. The output Y usually refers to the labels or values we're aiming to predict.

- The Big Job of Training Algorithms: The main job of a training algorithm is to build a model. This model's task is to figure out the relationship between input X and output Y. Once it's got that down, this model can be used to make predictions on new, unseen data.

- Good Data for the Win: What is the real secret to a top-notch machine learning system? High-quality, relevant data. The data used for training is like the road map for the predictions made by the machine learning model. So, any glitches or biases in the original data can lead to off-base or skewed predictions.

- Playing With Decision Trees: Decision trees are a pretty straightforward pick in the machine learning model toolshed for making predictions. They're a lot like a flowchart, guiding you down different paths through a bunch of questions until you reach an answer.

- Steering Clear of Overfitting: In machine learning, it's crucial to steer clear of overfitting. This happens when a model is so good at memorizing the training data, it doesn't do so well with new data. The trick is finding that sweet spot between how complex the model is and how much data there is.

- Training Algorithms Across the Board: The concept of setting up a model class and then using a training algorithm to find the best fit isn't just true for one machine learning model. It applies to different models, including regression analysis and neural networks.

Programming Through Data

The competitive weapon of every organization in this era is data.

Working With Data

This chapter's big question is: how do we choose the right kind of data to make the best model? Is our data a treasure chest full of gold, or is it more like a Pandora's box? How can we make sure our data is top-notch in order to build flawless models? It's kind of like programming, but instead of code, we're dealing with data.

Our training algorithm is like a supersmart GPS, using the data we give it to make the best route. Remember those trees we made from our original data? Each one could give a different price for a new house.

The training algorithm's job was to check out all the possible trees, see how they did, and pick the best ones. The amount of data we have is crucial for this. If we don't have enough data, we might lose confidence in our models—this is something we call *overfitting*. For example, one of our trees looked really promising, but it didn't have enough data, so its predictions were a bit shaky.

So, what can we do? One simple step could be to get more data. With this new data, we can make better trees and feel more confident in our predictions. Having more data might also change the way we think about errors. Previously, we liked the first tree because it was simple, and it had balanced data. But with all the new data, we might start to like the third tree more, even though it's more complicated.

This isn't just about our trees. It's a general rule for machine learning; if you have more data, you can make more complex rules. If you don't have much data, you might have to stick to simple models, like linear regression, which only draws straight lines. But if you have lots of data, your models can get more complex and handle more complicated rules.

This connection between how much data you have and how complex your models can be stays the same, no matter what kind of model you're working with. So, we need to ask ourselves; does our data really reflect the thing we're making predictions for?

Both the amount and quality of your data are highly important when figuring out how relevant it is to what you're trying to do. They both have a big effect on how strong your data is and, in turn, how reliable your model's predictions are.

The Significance of Data Diversity

Let's take a look at the importance of the way our data represents what we want to study. This is crucial because it changes how much we can rely on our model's predictions. Before we even start putting our model together, we need to check if the data we've got can give us predictions we can trust. This really shows how important it is to have good, representative data.

Aiming for perfect representation in a dataset might seem like a pipe-dream. What really matters, and needs some serious thought, is how big the gap is between the data we have and the data we wish we had. Figuring out these differences is essential, and, usually, it's something we learn from real-world observations and a bit of trial and error. To make sure it's worth the time and effort spent on building a model from a certain dataset, we need to have a rough idea of what the data might tell us, even if it's not 100 percent perfect.

Nailing this isn't just about being a data guru; it's mostly about knowing what you're trying to do and where your data came from. That's why, we have to ask ourselves how well our training data represents what we want to study. The answer might often be "not very well," but the key thing here is figuring out how far off our current data is from our dream data.

But there's another big thing to think about: how good your data is and how much of it you have. Looking at the variables, or *columns*, in your dataset is just as important as counting the data points, or *rows*. Sure, having more data points can be a good thing, but what about the quality of the data? Can adding more or better variables make our predictions more accurate?

Imagine, instead of just saying a song is *fast* or *slow*, we know its exact beats per minute (BPM). And, we've added other stuff like when the song was released or what genre it is. Here, we're trying to boost our data with more specific information to increase the chances of making a better model.

So, what changes does this make to our model? Firstly, it makes it easier to tell the difference between hits and flops. Secondly, it lets us break down the data in more ways, which could make our model's predictions more precise.

However, this brings up a tricky question: how do we decide whether it's better we need more data or better quality data? While it might be easier to understand the benefits of having more data, figuring out how useful it will be to add more variables can be a bit harder. Predicting the impact of a variable we haven't measured yet, like the song's genre, requires a bit of guesswork and an eye for spotting what might finetune a prediction.

Tailoring Data Relevance and Quality for Pinpoint Predictions

Adding more details, or columns, to your dataset can seriously level up your prediction game. But don't forget—simply tossing in more data isn't some magic solution. The real power move is in the quality and relevance of the added information. For example, knowing a user's e-mail provider might expand your dataset, but it doesn't really help predict their music preference. So, packing your dataset with variables isn't the secret to a killer model. Instead, you should aim to enrich your dataset with meaningful, relevant information, which is more about creativity and intuition than just data collection.

Now, let's think about how we convert real-world characteristics into input variables. This isn't a foolproof process, and you're bound to miss some stuff. Sure, you might jot down things like a user's favorite artists or most listened-to genres, but you might overlook other important details. Aspects like listening times, the kind of device used for streaming, or even the user's location can really affect their playlist preferences, but they might not find their way into your dataset.

Regardless of how much effort you put in, your dataset will always be a bit incomplete because translating the real world into data means losing some information. Recognizing these gaps and understanding their implications is critical. For example, if your model doesn't account for the time a user typically listens to music, it might struggle when trying to predict playlists for night owls or early birds. Depending on the size of these gaps, they might influence how you interpret your model's predictions, or even whether you find these predictions trustworthy.

So, to tie it all together, when you're building a model, you need to think beyond just identifying the inputs. You should also consider what relevant parts of the real world your data might be overlooking. This broader perspective will help you to construct a more comprehensive predictive model.

Understanding Key Ideas and Why They Matter

As we dig deeper, we bump into this key idea of layered systems. It's all about learning smaller concepts step by step. It might feel like we're suddenly changing the subject, but this is a key idea to get your head around. Most of the time, complex tasks are actually a bunch of smaller tasks all happening together.

There are a couple of main ways to include these smaller tasks in machine learning models. You could make a separate model for each task, but that would mean you need data for each one. Or you could design the models so that they learn to do these tasks on their own.

These two ways are different approaches to figuring out the smaller tasks. The first way puts the responsibility on the people designing the system to identify and teach these tasks, while the second way lets the model learn and figure out the tasks on its own.

Each way has its pros and cons. Teaching the smaller tasks directly means you need a good understanding of the tasks and the right data. You can check how the system's doing at each stage, but you might miss out on important tasks you didn't know about.

On the other hand, letting the system learn on its own gives it more flexibility, but it might need more data. It also means you can't see how well the model's doing, especially for tasks like spotting pedestrians.

For example, music recommendation systems like Spotify's Discover Weekly use this self-learning approach. Instead of defining music genres in advance, the system learns and figures out its own smaller tasks. This way, it's been successful in finding unique features of a song, like vibrato singing or bass drums, that an audio engineer might not have specifically pointed out.

This shows how powerful and efficient machine learning algorithms can be when they're allowed to learn their own smaller tasks. Understanding these smaller tasks and how to use them in machine learning opens up new opportunities to get the most out of your data, leading to more accurate and advanced predictive models. It shows that, in machine learning, both the final goal and the steps required to get there—or the final result and the smaller tasks—are essential.

Gathering Quality Data

Let's get into the nuances of data acquisition and how the presence of quality data can steer the types of problems we aim to resolve with AI. This concept is applicable even when we're dealing with generative AI, which appears to generate outputs such as text or images from thin air. In reality, the intricacy of creating these generative AI systems is tied to a specific part of the process—the finetuning. The challenge here lies in the supervised learning aspect; acquiring apt input–output pairs that embody the problem we seek to solve.

Whether it's decision making, prediction models, or even generative AI, there's a universal process. Data is fed into a training algorithm, which yields a model. The model then generates predictions. The segment we'll be focusing on is the data acquisition. The data we obtain doesn't just fortuitously represent everything we want. Instead, there's an art to the process of data collection; the quality and nature of this data subsequently influence the tasks we decide to undertake.

A vital point to underline is that AI only has access to the data provided, not the wider context of the world. In any task, it's important to ensure the relevant information is encoded into the data that will be used by a supervised learning system. Anything that is not included in the data, any information that you fail to capture, won't magically appear in the model. AI systems don't have inherent contextual understanding; they only see what is directly presented through the data.

By understanding and implementing these insights, we can optimize our data-gathering processes and better inform the types of problems we direct our AI systems to solve. As a next step, let's work on some practical tasks in order to apply and reinforce these concepts.

The Complexity of Detecting Scams

One big issue that has been causing many large companies a lot of concern is the detection of scams in the world of online shopping. As online purchasing becomes increasingly commonplace for everything from everyday essentials to major household items, the challenge of distinguishing fraudulent transactions from legitimate ones has grown significantly.

At first glance, you might think, "Let's use AI to solve this." The approach seems quite straightforward—gather a vast amount of transaction data, identify the questionable transactions, train a machine learning model with this labeled data, and voila, you have an automated system capable of flagging potential scams. Many financial institutions and digital payment platforms are indeed moving in this direction, with hopes of developing a machine learning-based solution to mitigate the risk of online scams.

But it quickly becomes apparent that there are numerous obstacles on this path. One significant hurdle is deciding how to label the transactions. Who determines which transactions are potentially fraudulent? On what basis are they making this judgment? Are they conducting an exhaustive investigation of each transaction, or are they making quick decisions based on superficial patterns?

Now, consider this: if the individuals tasked with identifying scams cannot agree on what constitutes a scam, then the machine learning model trained on this inconsistent data will be equally uncertain. Unlike predicting whether it will rain tomorrow, where everyone can agree on what constitutes rain, labels for potentially fraudulent transactions are highly subjective, making it extremely challenging to build a universally accepted model.

To add to the complexity, scams are constantly evolving. Fraudsters continually adapt their tactics, becoming ever more sophisticated and difficult to detect. This dynamic nature of online scams complicates the detection process even further.

Although detecting online scams may initially seem like a simple matter of data collection and processing, the underlying issues are far more intricate. They involve the delicate task of identifying which transactions are potentially fraudulent, as well keeping up with as the rapidly changing nature of scammer tactics. In summary, detecting online scams is about more than just crunching numbers; it's a complex puzzle that requires astute and adaptable solutions.

Imagine an online scam claiming that a popular e-commerce site is offering a 95 percent discount for the next hour only. This could be a real, limited-time promotional event, or it could be a fraudulent attempt to ambush unsuspecting shoppers. An AI system trained on past data has no way of distinguishing between these two scenarios—it doesn't have real-time insight into the e-commerce site's current promotional activities. Similarly, if a scammer creates a false narrative about new shipping regulations causing major delays, the AI system cannot verify this claim using only past data.

This reliance on past data is a fundamental limitation of AI. Pattern-matching based on historical data doesn't provide valuable insight into current or future events. And this isn't a limitation that can be addressed simply by obtaining more or better data. It's a fundamental aspect of how AI works, and it's important to recognize this when setting expectations for AI-based solutions.

Here's the key point: transforming real-world events into datasets can limit what we can achieve with AI. You might think, "I want an AI system that can accurately detect online scams," and that seems reasonable. After all, a team of human experts could examine individual transactions and identify potential scams, so why couldn't an AI system do the same?

The challenge lies in the nature of the data required for training AI systems. While human experts have access to a vast array of contextual information, AI systems can only learn from the specific data they're given. Therefore, the task that seems straightforward for humans may be extremely difficult, or even impossible, for AI.

Therefore, even tasks that appear feasible and straightforward may need to be adjusted or redefined when we're planning to use AI to tackle them. This isn't a shortcoming of the technology, but a reflection of the fundamental nature of machine learning—its reliance on historical data to make predictions about the present or future.

Unmasking Scams to Exposing Bots

Let's take another look at this from a different angle. Rather than trying to single out every scam in the digital universe, many platforms have decided to take a step back and focus on a broader target: the bots behind the scams. It turns out that this is a slightly less complicated mission because there's more consensus on what qualifies an account as a bot.

Think about it like this: imagine an online platform has a special screening test when creating an account. Let's say it requires solving a small puzzle or answering a question that demands human-like thinking and response, something beyond a bot's capabilities. This method can potentially be used to label accounts as *bot* or *not a bot* based on their performance in this test.

What we're doing here is a bit of a pivot. Instead of being knee-deep in the question of whether this an online scam or not, we're shifting toward another, more straightforward question: "Is this account operated by a bot?" It's usually less tricky to collect reliable data on bot activity, compared to identifying scams.

However, remember, we're tackling a slightly different issue here. If our goal was detecting scams, our instinctive response would be to take down the content as soon as it's flagged as a scam. But, with bot detection, the response could be different. Perhaps we restrict the activities of the bot account, maybe we limit its reach instead of taking it down completely. There's a range of responses possible because, at the end of the day, we're solving a different problem.

So here's the golden rule: you've got a problem you want to solve (scam detection), and then there's this adjacent, less complicated problem (bot detection). The game is all about identifying this adjacent problem, solving it effectively, and using it as a proxy to achieve what you wanted to achieve with the original problem.

In Summary

AI can't untangle the messy debates we humans have. And believe it or not, sometimes it makes things even worse. It can blanket our disputes under the supposed *fairness* of a machine learning system. You might not agree with the person setting up the labels, but once the task is passed through the AI, who's left to argue with? You might just assume that machine learning is neutral and correct, when in reality, it's just echoing the labels you initially disagreed with. So, when someone tells you they've got an AI fix for an issue that sparks different opinions among people, it's wise to be a bit skeptical. There's a good chance they're just sweeping some disagreement under the carpet.

Another problem you might run into is the difficulty of precisely defining what you're trying to predict. We may have a basic understanding of the output we desire, but turning that into a quantifiable column that fits into a dataset ... that's a real challenge. This issue isn't just limited to detecting scams or identifying bots; it also extends to somewhat nebulous notions like creditworthiness or qualifications. Sure, it'd be fantastic if we could get AI to predict who's a qualified applicant. But that's not exactly the same as the actual variable that's going to pop up in your dataset. The idea of being *qualified* exists out there in the real world. The label Y in your dataset is just a piece of data. They're not the same thing.

This problem has a structure to it. The question is: how can we morph a generic output into something we can actually measure? And if we were to attempt to translate this question into professional machine-understandable jargon, we might attempt to ask it this way: How does your dataset label (Y) differ from the actual outcome you want? If you want to detect a *qualified* applicant, what did you actually measure? If you want to identify *scams*, what did you actually measure? Recognizing these discrepancies is vital because it shows us what we're leaving out when we build a system.

Key Takeaways

- Getting Data Ready for Decision Trees: When a process will involve building decision trees, you need to think about both how much data you have and how good it is. More data lets you make more complex models, while having better and more relevant variables gives you more detailed insights.
- Having Data That's a Good Representation: You need to make sure the data you're using for your model is a good

reflection of the situation you're making predictions for. Understanding any differences between the perfect data and the data you actually have is super important.

- Making Your Data More Predictive: Adding more specific variables to your data can make your predictions better. You might need to swap out broad categories for exact measurements or bring in new variables that are likely to change the results.

- Finding the Right Mix of Data Quantity and Quality: Adding more data can be a good thing, but you need to make sure this extra data is good quality and relevant. Simply adding more variables doesn't make your model better, unless those variables give useful, predictive insights.

- Recognizing That Your Data Isn't Perfect: When you turn real-world phenomena into data, you can lose some information. Knowing this fact can help you spot possible systematic errors in your model and guide the way you understand your model's predictions.

- Using Layers in Machine Learning Systems: Complex tasks often depend on smaller tasks or concepts. There are two main ways to include these in machine learning models; you can make a specific model for each task or make models that learn these tasks on their own.

- Choosing Flexibility or Tradeoffs When Teaching Smaller Tasks: Both ways of including smaller tasks in machine learning models have their pros and cons. Teaching tasks directly allows you to check how well the model is doing, but you might miss out on important tasks. On the other hand, letting the model learn on its own can result in more flexible models, but it might need more data and make it harder to see how well the model's doing.

- Letting Models Learn Smaller Tasks on Their Own: Sometimes, machine learning algorithms can be more powerful and efficient when they're allowed to learn their own smaller tasks. This means they can spot and use different parts of the data that a human might not have specifically pointed out.

Generative AI and Language Models

What large language models have done, is fur-
ther democratized access to deep computation.

The Tale of Generative AI and Its Transformative Power

If you've been hearing the buzz around generative AI and wondering what all the fuss is about, you're in the right place. In this chapter, we're going to unpack generative AI. We'll start from its early days, look at how it's grown, and think about where it might be headed.

To really understand AI as it is now, we need to go back in time, follow its journey from the very start, and see how its growth has gone hand in hand with the evolution of the ways we do business. The boom we're seeing in AI isn't just about tech getting better; it's also a reflection of us growing as a society.

We're going to look at the big changes generative AI is bringing to all sorts of sectors. We'll shine a light on game-changers like DALL·E, an image generator that's changing the world of design, and ChatGPT, a text generator that can chat like a human. These supercool tech advances aren't just pushing our creativity to new levels; they're kickstarting an era of innovation that we couldn't have dreamed of before.

As we get into the nitty-gritty of AI's development, we'll unpack the transformation from simple AI models to complex systems that really get the context. You'll see how AI has gone from basic setups that made predictions from a set of data to advanced models that can learn, interpret, and come up with new, but still relevant, results.

By the end of this chapter, you'll have a good handle on where generative AI started, and what it's like now. You will thus be ready to think about where it could go in the future. With this in your toolkit, you'll be set to bring generative AI into your work life, make the most of its principles, and dive into its endless possibilities. With this fresh viewpoint, you'll be ready to actively shape the future of this rapidly changing field and escalate how you do things in our fast-paced digital world.

Igniting Growth and Innovation
With a Powerful Ally

Imagine you're running a business and you're about to roll out this really cool, innovative new product. There's the excitement of doing something new, but let's be honest, there's also that little knot of doubt. You've got an amazing team, a solid plan, and you've put your resources where they need to be. But trying to predict exactly what's going to happen? That can feel like trying to see through a dense fog. So what if you had a super tool on your side—a generative AI sidekick that can give you valuable insights, spot trends, and even help you with the creative part of your product development?

This isn't a sneak preview of the future; it's what's happening right now. Generative AI is shaking up creative processes in all kinds of industries, showing its worth as a partner in sparking new ideas. Groundbreaking models like DALL·E and ChatGPT show us that generative AI isn't just about number-crunching and predicting things; it's about being a part of the creative process.

At this point, you might be thinking, "So where does generative AI fit into my business? Is it just another tech gimmick, or could it really shake up the way we solve problems and build strategies?" Those are good questions, and they deserve some serious thought. To answer them, let's compare it to something we all get—how markets evolve.

Just like any emerging market trend, generative AI didn't just appear out of thin air. It's been years in the making, with lots of trial and error, and constant innovation—pretty much like any game-changing product or service in today's market. Understanding how it's evolved can help you make the most of its potential and sidestep the pitfalls that often trip up folks who get on board early.

Instead of traditional AI models that just process input data to predict an outcome, generative AI actually interacts with the information, learns from it, and creates totally new outputs, like a sentence or an image. This isn't a sudden jump, but a natural progression in the overall story of AI.

The growth of generative AI is similar to a successful product launch. You need advanced tech, useful customer data, and a wise use of resources. In the same way, technological breakthroughs, the availability of huge amounts of data, and a boost in computational power have all put generative AI center stage. These have cleared the way for us to do generative tasks on a much bigger scale—kind of like taking your business global.

The Story of Language Models

To understand the beginnings of generative AI and language models, we need to time travel back to the 1940s. In those days, the idea of statistical language modeling was as ground-breaking as AI is in some sectors today. One pioneering brain behind this transformative concept was the brilliant mathematician Claude Shannon. The same Claude Shannon of Bell Telephone Laboratories, who also contributed to the seminal 1956 Dartmouth College research with John McCarthy, discussed in earlier chapters.

Shannon started his journey with a basic but powerful concept, envisioning English as a system made up of 26 characters and spaces, generated randomly. This idea is similar to the birth of a business idea—raw and somewhat tangled, but signifying the start of something significant.

Through careful refinement and iterative adjustments based on feedback, Shannon's model started showing promise. Identifying the sequence of characters, he made considerable progress toward creating text that seemed somewhat realistic. This is similar to a business finetuning its product to better meet market demands.

The cycle of refining the model, shifting from characters to words, is like a business scaling up its operations. Shannon showed that by predicting the next word based on the previous one, he could put together a sequence of English words. While these sentences lacked logical coherence, they still looked a lot like English. Despite the computational limitations of his time, Shannon's foresight paved the way for today's language models.

Let's dig deeper now to understand how language models, like AI chatbots, work. Picture a gigantic spreadsheet, spreading 100,000 words wide and shooting up to an astounding height of 10^{20}. Each cell represents a tiny possibility within a vast sea of potential word sequences. It's a mind-boggling idea, right?

However, this method turns out to be impractical. Think about tracking not just three, but 20 previous words. All of a sudden, the potential combinations exceed the total number of atoms in the known universe! This daunting challenge underscores the limitations of Claude Shannon's early methodology.

So, are we missing something vital here? What if we could enrich raw data with our knowledge of English grammar rules? This suggestion sparks a long-standing debate within the AI community: should we rely mainly on data, or should we also incorporate our understanding of the underlying rules? Judging by the path of supervised machine learning, it appears the data-centric approach is winning the race. Generative AI seems to be following a similar route: let the data tell the tale, and the rules will gradually reveal themselves.

To provide more context, let's rewind to the 1960s and meet ELIZA, a basic program created at MIT under the guidance of Professor Joseph Weizenbaum (who ironically was a critic of AI, but that's for another book). ELIZA, an early conversational agent, could respond to statements like, "I'm concerned about the global warming crisis," with generic replies such as, "Tell me more about the global warming crisis." ELIZA was at its core a client-centered therapist and could engage in basic conversations by rephrasing the user's statements as questions. Despite its simple design, users attributed a surprising level of intelligence to ELIZA—an aspect of AI that has increasingly become accepted as the standard over time.

The Leap to Sophisticated Models

The creation of more complex language models has been possible due to the perfect blend of data-driven techniques and rule-based methods. This balance has given birth to intelligent assistants like Siri and Google Duplex. However, until recently, these models had limited reach and remained largely out of reach for the average user.

Today, the landscape is changing at a rate we've never seen before, with models like OpenAI's GPT pushing generative AI into the spotlight.

Fundamentally, these contemporary generative models operate on the principle outlined by Shannon. They predict the next word based on a few preceding ones, much like your smartphone's auto-complete feature.

To put it in simpler terms, think of GPT as an AI that enhances your phone's suggested next word functionality but considers hundreds of previous words instead of just a couple. This text generation process is a series of individual predictions about the most likely next word, each contributing to a cohesive piece of text. So, we find ourselves back at our starting point: the captivating world of generative AI.

However, it's important to clear up a common misconception at this point. ChatGPT and GPT are not the same, and understanding the differences between them can shed light on how these models work. ChatGPT typically uses a GPT-3 model, or GPT-4, or any subsequent version. This model has been tweaked to give ChatGPT its conversational abilities, rather than just predicting the next word. But at its heart, it's all about predicting what comes next.

GPT, the cornerstone of language modeling, isn't exclusive to a specific entity. Through certain modifications or *finetuning*, GPT has been adjusted to create ChatGPT, making it more suitable for everyday conversation. While the core concept has been around for a while, adapting a model for public use as a chatbot required extra work. But the principle remains: predicting the next character, step by step.

This process starts with a sentence like "I'm having an awesome day." Each subsequence becomes a data point for training. If *awesome* is the input, *day* is the output. Repeating this process generates countless training examples from a single sentence, each forming a unique input–output pair.

GPT's training data is sourced from various places, including Web texts, Wikipedia, and more. Transformed into machine-readable *tokens*, the model trains on hundreds of billions of words. But at its core, it's all about predicting what comes next.

The Delicate Interplay of Chance and Skill in Generative AI

One important fact to understand about GPT is that it doesn't just spit out the likeliest word. Instead, it assigns odds to a range of words, and its choice reflects these probabilities. For example, if there's a 50-50 shot the next word is *essential* or *crucial*, it will make a toss-up pick based on these odds. This touch of unpredictability means that if it were asked to repeat the task, it might make a different choice each time, injecting a pinch of creativity into the mix.

While these models are rooted in supervised machine learning, as we've touched on, they demand a hefty amount of engineering wizardry to be fully operational. We've advanced a great deal from Shannon's original method, cooking up complex systems that handle sophistication in a far more efficient manner.

Understanding how these models tick helps us critically evaluate claims about their deep comprehension or intelligence. While GPT might not genuinely understand text the way a human does, its predictive prowess is hard to question. It's processed more text than any human could ever get through—but this doesn't mean it boasts superior knowledge or understanding. We need to remember that human and machine intelligence function on fundamentally different scales. GPT might be a pro at predicting the next word in a sequence, but it doesn't *know* more about a subject than a human does.

GPT to ChatGPT

Turning GPT into a conversational AI like ChatGPT is achieved by *fine-tuning*. When it comes to cooking up an AI model, the process kicks off by crafting a sturdy next-word predictor like GPT, using a ton of Internet texts and the most robust computational power we've got. Getting these models trained demands a hefty investment of resources and time, with products like GPT calling for years of computational work and serious funding. At present, only a handful of organizations have the capacity to shoulder this resource-hungry task, leading to a bit of centralization in model training.

Once GPT has been well developed, the next step is to morph it into something more specialized, like ChatGPT. The trick here is to carefully craft a task-specific dataset for the goal you're chasing. For instance, if you're gunning to create a chatbot, you'd generate likely chatbot questions and answers, creating a manageable dataset for extra refining. For tasks in specialized fields, like legal analysis, the base GPT model might not cut it. However, with a curated dataset of legal questions and answers, you can finetune the model to boost its performance in your area.

This finetuning process involves gradually refining the model based on the task-specific dataset, building on GPT's sturdy foundation. The process starts with a ton of Internet text and the original next-word predictor. From this vast body, a smaller, more focused dataset is extracted. This dataset is then put through a finetuning algorithm that mirrors the initial training algorithm, resulting in a model specifically refined for the task at hand. This strategy allows for the creation of task-specific models that need a much smaller dataset compared to the original GPT training dataset.

In the case of ChatGPT, a unique dataset made up of interactive prompts and responses is used. Starting with the GPT model, the model goes through several stages of finetuning to eventually churn out ChatGPT. This finetuning process epitomizes the delicate art of moving from a broad predictive AI model to a more focused and effective conversational AI.

The Task of Refinement

Imagine you've got access to ChatGPT, but you're looking to customize it to better fit your unique needs. What's the game plan? You could feed it extra data, with the kinds of questions and answers you like, giving the model a nudge to whip up responses that align more closely with your personal preferences. But this isn't as straightforward as it first sounds. Basically, you're throwing a few curveballs into the original GPT training examples, and, as you add more examples, the model starts to line up more with your target results. This extra data gently nudges the model's focus from just guessing the next word to guessing it in a way that matches your desired response more accurately.

Now, considering the effort needed to curate a specialized dataset, why even bother with the giant task of creating a huge word predictor in the first place? The reason lies in the vast volume of data available for next word prediction, an amount far larger than what could be gathered for a specific task like a chatbot. Moreover, creating the base model isn't a solo mission—there are groups already pouring resources into this effort. Even if not all the data used for next word prediction directly relates to your specific task, it sets a solid foundation. By being ace at predicting the next word, the model learns to spit out grammatically correct text, a skill that needs a lot of time and data to pick up. This gives you a stepping stone from which you can guide the model toward completing your specific task. The key takeaway here is that a large heap of somewhat relevant data, paired with a small chunk of high-quality, task-specific data, tends to beat a smaller chunk of high-quality data on its own. This principle underpins applications like Harvey, OpenAI's legal analysis tool, and the popular ChatGPT—both harness the power of finetuning.

Mixing these two different types of data is a key balancing act—it's about finding the sweet spot between the general and the specific. This lets you craft a dynamic, refined intelligence that can roll with various situations. The blend of a broad knowledge base and a tightly curated set of specifics drives the progress of technologies like Harvey and ChatGPT, allowing them to consistently knock it out of the park. It's this meeting between the expansive and the specific that arms these tools with their impressive skills. This balance truly encapsulates the thrilling evolution of AI, morphing it from a simple text predictor into a generator of insightful dialogue.

Navigating Knowledge in the Digital Maze

In today's complex digital landscape, we often find ourselves in a peculiar catch-22. We're swimming in an ocean of information, but trying to find the exact bits we need, when we need them can feel like hunting for a needle in a haystack. In any buzzing company, countless chats happen daily across various channels like Slack, e-mails, or shared docs. These chats create a massive pool of knowledge, experiences, and clever answers to all sorts of problems. Sadly, this information often gets lost in the mix, becoming forgotten bits of yesterday.

Let's picture a new employee who hops onto a project midway. She runs into a technical roadblock that she believes has been solved before. In a typical setting, she might have to dig through a pile of old threads or rely on her coworkers' memories for relevant information. This could lead to her spending tons of time rediscovering the solution, instead of driving her work forward. This situation puts a spotlight on a common hurdle—the challenge of effectively using a company's collective memory.

Language models, trained on a vast spread of text, can churn out responses that are spot-on for user queries given the context. When these models absorb a company's communication data, they basically serve as a live, intelligent, searchable archive. Our hypothetical new employee could ask her question to this AI model, which would use its training from the company's internal chats to quickly pull up a discussion from, let's say, two years ago, about the same technical issue.

What's crucial is that these models get context, not just keywords. They can provide a more nuanced response than your average keyword search tool, delivering a precise answer along with the related conversation for better understanding.

However, deploying these models brings up some important considerations. Issues of data privacy and confidentiality become absolutely critical. The company needs to make sure it has strong data anonymization steps and permission structures in place before training the model on internal chats.

The use of language models offers a powerful way to unlock the information tucked away in a company's internal communications. It turns archived chats into a dynamic, accessible knowledge base, effectively using the company's collective memory. This use case shows one of the many game-changing ways AI can be used, where language models help us solve the mind-blowing paradox of plenty that defines our digital age.

As we travel through the world of AI and language models, we see that every step, from Shannon's foundational theories to today's advanced models, is a celebration of human creativity. It's a reminder that our quest to decode, understand, and mimic human language is far from over. Instead, we're in an exciting era where every discovery, every model, and every refined application brings us one step closer to understanding the deep connection between language, knowledge, and the human experience.

Key Takeaways

- The Magic of Generative AI: Generative AI models like GPT work their magic by predicting the next word in a sequence.

This skill is their secret sauce, letting them create coherent and meaningful text.

- Probability Theory is at the Core: These AI models rest on the foundations of probability theory and machine learning, concepts initially unveiled by Claude Shannon. They guess the next word based on the probabilities they've learned from heaps of training data.

- Language Models as Time Capsules: Language models like GPT-3 are a bit like condensed time capsules of the Internet at the time they were trained. They mix and mash existing data, but they don't come up with brand new information.

- The Journey of Refinement: The journey from a broad language model like GPT to a more specialized one like ChatGPT is guided by a refining process called *finetuning*. This process uses a task-specific dataset to tweak the general model for a particular use.

- Walking the Line Between General and Specific Data: The finetuning process walks a fine line between a lot of somewhat relevant data and a smaller amount of high-quality, task-specific data. This balance sets the stage for dynamic models that can be adapted to different contexts.

- Unlocking Organizational Memory: Language models can tap into a company's collective memory by learning from its internal communications, turning it into a living, accessible knowledge base. But this strategy has to be implemented while strictly sticking to data privacy and confidentiality standards.

- Getting to Know Language Models: Understanding how language models work lets us critically evaluate their strengths and weaknesses. While they're insanely good at predicting, they don't truly understand or know stuff in the way humans do.

Identifying Opportunities With AI

Driving efficiency in the enterprise is going to be a big opportunity ahead.

The Lens of Objectives

Automation

Starting on the Right Foot

If you're someone who's always curious about the next big thing in your industry, you've probably been amazed by what a real game-changer AI can be. It's clear that it has enormous potential to boost efficiency and take your operations to a whole new level. But the million-dollar question is, where do you start? How do you identify the objectives that are not only ready for automation but that also exist where AI can make a serious impact? In this chapter, we're going to show you how to find these golden opportunities, point out objectives that are crying out for automation, and highlight the incredible benefits AI brings.

Let's use an example to shed some light on this. Imagine a key job in the music industry—the talent scout. This person has a critical role in record companies, identifying and signing new artists. They need to sift through tons of demos and live performances, ensuring the potential artists tick all the boxes before getting a record deal. Just picture the pile of demos and gig recordings, all waiting for the thumbs up from our talent scout.

Here's the magic phrase—"tick all the boxes." What does this mean? Essentially, these are rules like having a unique sound or a solid fanbase that decide who gets a record deal. Now, at first glance, you might think this job is perfect for automation. After all, these rules seem simple enough to turn into a computer program. Traditional programming methods, where these rules are set out clearly, could help figure out whether a potential artist ticks all the boxes.

But here's where it gets interesting. There are different ways to describe what we want from this system. One way could be, "Y = meet specific talent requirements," an output that traditional programming can handle pretty well. However, we could also describe it as "Y = the talent scout's decision to sign." This is where machine learning really comes into its own. We can use old data and past decisions made by talent scouts to train a machine learning system. To make it even more impressive, we could define Y as "the artist's song becomes a hit"—the sort of task machine learning excels at.

Now, let's take a moment to consider the subtle differences between the last two scenarios. To get this, we need to revisit our earlier discussions about prediction and automation. In prediction, the situation dictates the outcome, like whether a song will become a hit. The outcome is a future event that unfolds over time. By contrast, automation lets us, the human operators, control the outcome based on the information we have right now. For example, a talent scout decides to sign an artist after carefully evaluating their potential.

So, what kind of tasks are mature for automation? They usually involve a repetitive process where you look at an X (like a demo) to make a Y decision (like a record deal). Ideally, these tasks would have a lot of data, and automating them would bring real benefits, like saving time or freeing up resources. Automating the job of a talent scout, for instance, could free up resources that could be better utilized elsewhere.

The main point is, X could be anything, as long as it's clearly defined and measurable. We can build a dataset around it or use standard digital formats like audio or video. The key part of Y is that it's a human judgment, just like talent scout's decision to sign an artist. The catch is, this judgment should be based solely on X, the input data. If it depends on additional information not included in X, then that part of the task might be hard to automate, because we don't have access to this external data.

And this isn't just about talent scouting; it's about spotting any potential areas for automation in your operations. By viewing roles through this lens, you can identify objectives where AI could make a massive difference, where your operations could see major benefits. With this mindset, you're well equipped to kick off your AI projects, inspire change within your team, and disrupt your industry.

The Guiding Light

When you're ready to dive into the automation game, having some guidelines to help you figure out which tasks are right for automation can be extremely handy. A few years ago, there was a pretty neat rule of thumb: if a regular person can do a task in about a second, then it's ready for automation with AI. But while this rule might sound useful, it's not a one-size-fits-all deal. There are plenty of tasks that take more than a second that have parts that can be automated just fine. Let's take radiology as an example—a field where human involvement usually takes more than a quick second, but certain parts of the job can be automated nicely.

On the flip side, some tasks that take less than a second can be surprisingly tough to automate. Humor is a perfect example of this puzzle. For us humans, it might be a no-brainer, but automating humor is a big challenge. It needs a deep understanding of context, cultural differences, and even what's happening in the real world right now. Humor is a complex human experience, closely tied to our personal and cultural understanding of the world, making it a hard nut for automation to crack.

But it's key to remember that the world of AI is not stuck—it's always changing. With the rise of advanced big language models, our edge in understanding the world is slowly being chipped away. These models, having swallowed up a massive part of the Internet, are now armed with a huge amount of context, making the job of automating complex functions a bit less scary.

The main principle here is that, for a task to be ready for automation, the relationship between X and Y must meet three key criteria—stability, generality, and self-containment. The relationship needs to be stable, meaning it doesn't change drastically over time. This stability allows for predictability, which is key for automation. The relationship should also be general enough for different individuals to arrive at roughly the same relationship under different situations.

Lastly, the task needs to be self-contained. This means that all the required information to do the task is included in X, without needing to rely on outside information that we can't feed into the machine. In other words, the task can be done based solely on the available input data, without needing extra data or context outside its scope. If a task meets these criteria, it's more likely to be a good fit for successful automation.

Two Flavors of Automation

We need to distinguish between two main types of objectives that are fit for automation. Each of these objectives has unique characteristics and potential. Understanding their differences is the key to identifying opportunities for successful automation within your organization.

The first type of objective we're discussing involves replicating things that humans are already doing. The talent scout example we talked about is a great example of this category. The second type of objective is a bit more imaginative—it poses the question, what tasks would a human do if we were willing to pay them enough? This requires us to think beyond current roles and contemplate potential tasks that could be automated.

Let's take, for instance, AI apps that analyze a human's handwriting and transform it into a font. While it's technically feasible for a skilled human typographer to do this, it wouldn't make financial sense to pay a typographer hundreds of dollars to turn someone's handwriting into a single unique font. But it could be a wise investment to pay typographers to create a bunch of these fonts if we're planning to use them to train a machine learning system, which could then generate similar fonts at a fraction of the cost, or even for free.

This example demonstrates the critical idea that, when thinking about tasks for automation, we shouldn't restrict ourselves to just the tasks that are currently being done. Economic limitations might prevent certain tasks from being executed by humans, but AI automation can significantly reduce the cost, making these tasks feasible.

There are countless examples of tasks that fall into this category. A typographer could technically do what online font generators do, but it might not be worth their time. However, we could pay typographers to create a database of fonts that we could use to train an AI model. Consider something as commonplace as scanning barcodes at a grocery checkout—while nobody would hire a person to manually input each item's details, if we could gather enough training examples of barcode readings, we could train an AI system to manage this task effortlessly.

Another example might be a system that schedules your robotic vacuum cleaner to clean the house when you're expected to be away. It wouldn't be cost-effective to hire someone to keep an eye on your schedule and operate your vacuum cleaner accordingly, but it could be practical and cost-saving to automate this task.

This leads us to the second big takeaway in automation: We need to look beyond the tasks that are currently being done. Think about tasks that humans could technically do but don't, often because of economic limitations or other logistical challenges. Automation has the potential to make these tasks economically feasible, paving the way for increased efficiency and innovation.

The Potential of Automation

On the path to full-on automation, one worry tends to come up a lot: will this replace people's jobs? This worry has made people in the research world dig into which jobs are more or less likely to get hit by automation. There's a popular idea that automation will mostly affect folks with lower-paying jobs. To check this out, the researchers plotted wages on one axis and how well a job fits with machine learning on the other axis, with higher scores showing a bigger chance for automation. The results showed that the level of pay doesn't have a strong tie with how likely a job is to get automated. Jobs that are ready for automation can be found at all pay levels, suggesting that automation could affect a wide range of jobs, not just the ones with lower pay.

Despite what most people think, the results suggest that it's not really the wage levels that define about how well a job fits with machine learning. And, funnily enough, people with high-paying jobs might have more to worry about. This is because automating these high-paying jobs can lead to bigger returns on investment, which could speed up the move to automate these roles. When you look at individual jobs, it's clear that some are less ready for automation (like massage therapists, vets, and archaeologists), while others are more mature (like concierges, mechanical drafters, and even funeral directors). The job of funeral directors is a fascinating example because it's high on the automation list, mostly because of the paperwork involved, which is something that can easily be automated.

It's easy to be fooled when you look at a job as a single, static thing. Different parts of the same job can be more or less ready for automation. The work of a lawyer provides an interesting example. While some parts of a lawyer's job are complicated and tough to automate, a good chunk of their work is repetitive and could be ready for automation. For example, the discovery process involves going through loads of data to find relevant information, a task that's hard, repetitive work, and makes up 20 to 25 percent of the costs of a lawsuit. This part of a lawyer's job seems ready for automation and, indeed, there are already companies out there creating software to make the discovery process more efficient.

This brings us to our third big lesson about automation; we need to stop thinking about automating entire jobs and start focusing on automating specific tasks within jobs. Most jobs are too complex for a single machine learning system to fully automate. However, by pinpointing and automating individual tasks within jobs, we can see big gains in productivity and cost-saving.

So, our first rule of thumb for finding AI opportunities is to focus on tasks that can be automated. These could be tasks that people are currently doing, or tasks that they could potentially do. Your aim is to think about a task or part of someone's job that you think fits well with machine learning. It could be a task in health care, a specific part of a lawyer's job, or something entirely different. The challenge is in finding these tasks, figuring out how to collect quality data, and deciding how to separate a specific task from a job for automation.

By shifting our focus from automating entire jobs to automating specific tasks, we can balance the potential of machine learning with human skills, creating a future where AI enhances human labor rather than replacing it. We're on the brink of a thrilling era where technology is set to shake up our work lives, boost efficiency, and unlock amazing productivity. With an understanding of how to identify tasks that are ready for automation, we can make the most of the opportunities this revolution brings.

Prediction

Forecasting

In the last section, we dug into automation, talking about what it's good for and when it hits the mark. Now, we're about to jump into something just as intriguing but a bit different: the world of prediction. This will give us a better handle on the relationship between automation and prediction.

Let's kickstart this with some real-life examples where this stuff can really be useful, such as weather forecasting. It's extremely complex, but it's also a goldmine of opportunities for predictive models. Think about the number of people whose daily activities are influenced by weather changes. These folks could spend hours guessing what the weather will be like, which is where predictive tools can lend a hand.

The meteorologists have the tricky job of deciding what the weather's going to be like. Is it going to rain? Will there be a storm? How hot is it going to be? Their decisions rely on tons of variables, like temperature, humidity, wind speed, and so on. So basically, they need to predict two things: what the weather will be (weather prediction) and how it will affect daily activities (impact prediction).

Before we dive deeper into prediction, let's imagine how we could automate this process. We could use inputs like historical weather data, current atmospheric conditions, and other relevant details. The output, our target Y, would be the meteorologist's decision—to predict rain or sunshine. The training data for this automation model would be past weather records.

But, here's the catch. This automation approach sounds straightforward, but it's full of difficulties. Weather prediction depends on a ton of factors, which can make the data unpredictable and confusing for an automated system. Automation is great when things are steady and predictable, which isn't really the case here. Moreover, bias can further complicate these predictions. Even the best meteorologists can be influenced by all sorts of things, from past experiences to gut feelings. Ethical worries about weather prediction add even more uncertainty to using automation.

Given these challenges, it looks like automation might not be the best fit for weather prediction. So, we switch gears to prediction. We stick with the same input variables, but change the output to a prediction of what the weather will be like and its potential impact. The training data comes from historical weather records. This shift toward prediction offers a promising alternative to using technology to improve the complex world of weather forecasting.

But, just as with automation, this route isn't without its bumps. One big issue is the so-called one-sided or selective labels problem. This means there's a built-in bias in the data because outcomes are only observed for weather conditions that have previously occurred. This means our training data is a biased sample, which is a big challenge for creating successful predictive models.

Tackling Predictive Challenges in AI Applications

Now that we've set the stage for our predictive challenge, let's dive into some impediments that come up when we choose prediction over automation. Remember, if we'd gone with automation, we would just have tracked each meteorologist's weather forecast. But with prediction, we don't always see the actual weather event, because it depends on the meteorologist's forecast. So, while prediction has tons of potential, it also brings a unique hurdle that we wouldn't have encountered with automation.

When we're knee-deep in prediction tasks, we often bump into a common situation. Someone keeps guessing an outcome based on certain factors. The tricky part is figuring out how this person makes their guess. It might seem logical to turn this into an automation task since we can see the guessing process, which looks like it could be automated. But we switch to a prediction task when we have solid data, not just on the factors and the guess, but on the actual outcome.

If a meteorologist is guessing about the chance of rain, we might want to automate this guessing process. But if we have solid data on actual rainy days, we can skip automating the meteorologist's guess and predict the actual weather instead. This switch from an automation task, where our labels are guesses about an outcome, to a prediction task, where we have data about the outcome itself, is a major shift in the way we tackle the problem.

We've seen this switch work wonders in many situations. In weather forecasts, we predict the outcomes of rainfall, sunshine, or snow. In farming, we often predict crop productivity using harvest data, irrigation patterns, or pest infestations. For school closures, the prediction task could be estimating how severe the weather would have to be to cause a closure.

But these prediction tasks aren't without the selective labels problem we've mentioned. For example, we see data on crop yields for farms that went ahead with certain irrigation patterns but not for those who didn't.

This problem often pops up in prediction tasks because, while we can get data for all sorts of guesses, actual outcome data usually depends on the initial guess. This issue tends to show up when we switch from an automation problem to a prediction problem.

Prediction tasks also come up in areas like predicting natural disasters, where we predict a confirmed seismic activity or a hurricane path, or predicting energy consumption, where we predict usage spikes. These situations often stumble into the selective labels problem too. So, it's crucial to be aware of these challenges when deciding whether to use prediction as a tool to tackle your problem.

Prediction as a Partner in Decision Making

As we start to focus more on prediction instead of automation in real-life situations, we see a neat pattern showing up. Tools made for prediction usually aren't used directly to replace human decisions. Unlike automation, which aims to take over or speed up human decision making, prediction is often seen as a bonus in the decision-making process, usually improving the quality and depth of human judgments.

The habit of using predictive tools as helpers in making decisions, rather than complete substitutes, is common, especially in complicated systems like criminal justice. Judges often use predictions about the risk of the defendant not showing up or reoffending as key parts of their decision-making processes. Even though this approach might seem more complicated than just following what the machine says, it's generally seen as a better way to make decisions, which is why it's commonly used.

When we start using predictive tools, we pay a lot of attention to creating environments that support successful AI integration. Instead of just handing over a prediction to humans and letting them figure it out, a lot of effort goes into making sure these tools give an easily comprehensible interpretation of the results. They guide the user in understanding the predicted risks and comparing different probabilities.

How predictive tools are designed is extremely important and can really influence whether they work well or not. This involves not just getting high-quality data for prediction but also showing those predictions in a way that can help people.

Our journey started with looking for tasks that could be automated. But as we dive into the world of prediction, we need to remember its limitations, including the limits of the data we can see and the need to be careful that people don't rely too much on the predictions. A keen awareness of this helps keep human control and encourages the use predictions as valuable supplements to human judgment. The path might be twisty, but the potential benefits make it worth it. As we keep moving forward, let's keep exploring the ins and outs and opportunities within the worlds of automation and prediction.

The Lens of Data

Uncovering Value in Existing Data

The Potential of Existing Data

As we jump into data-driven strategies, we often find ourselves staring at a massive mountain of information that's already within our reach. The first step in our data adventure is figuring out how to unlock and make the most of the data we already have.

Imagine this: you're standing in front of a treasure trove of data, but you're not sure how to use it right. Getting hold of data often comes with huge challenges, like it not being available, headaches in collecting it, someone else owning it, legal roadblocks, and issues with merging different datasets. However, it's important to remember that many businesses might already be sitting on a heap of data they've gathered for other stuff.

Companies gather a lot of data as part of their everyday operations, especially in today's digital age where most transactions are done online. Often, this data isn't used to its max potential because its real value is hidden.

Consider Netflix, the streaming service, for example. They have a ton of data. This includes information about what shows are trending or which ones get abandoned mid-season. The value of such data is clear, as it can be used to predict viewing trends or sold to advertisers for a profit. But Netflix also has access to less obvious data. By simply monitoring the speed at which different shows are streamed, Netflix could collect important information about Internet speeds in various locations, a valuable bit of information for Internet service providers. The main takeaway here is that even a small effort in collecting data can unlock a lot of extra value.

The data you already have might be a goldmine that's just waiting to be discovered. Gathering detailed viewing data, for example, might be expensive or even illegal for some organizations, but a company like Netflix can easily get it from their existing resources. It might not be worth it for a company to monitor Internet speeds across cities, but for Netflix, whose service relies on these speeds, this is an added perk.

These uncharted opportunities exist whenever your position allows you to collect valuable data during your regular operations. For others, the cost of collecting this data might be too steep. The trick is to recognize these additional perks and use them to your advantage.

Consider Strava as another example. As an online fitness tracking platform offering tracking of runs, bike rides, and workouts, they have access to a heap of fitness data that could provide insights into how people are working out. But they're also collecting more than just fitness data. They might also be gathering useful information about users' locations, their preferred workout times, or even how much they interact with others on the platform. This secondary data could be extremely valuable, and it's being collected naturally as part of their main business operations.

So, the first step in our data-focused adventure involves realizing and using the hidden potential of the data we're already gathering. The untapped value in your existing data might surprise you, and finding it could kickstart a new era of growth and opportunity for your business.

Leveraging Data for More Than Originally Intended

Starbucks gives us a great illustration of this approach. They smartly repurposed customer order data into valuable tools for making predictions.

The trick often isn't just about using the existing data, but about subtly tweaking your product or service to gather specific data you're interested in. The online streaming industry is a fantastic example of this. Streaming platforms are sitting on a treasure trove of data: patterns of shows often watched together, trends in the popularity of certain genres, or even signs of online trends like viral challenges.

But how did streaming platforms manage to boost the value of their data so much? The answer is surprisingly simple: they introduced user profiles. Back when everyone was sharing a single profile, data was restricted to mixed, collective viewing habits. With the advent of user profiles, platforms were able to link views over time, effectively tracking the watching journey of individual viewers. This small adjustment significantly boosted the value of their data.

This strategy of making slight changes to bump up data collection is also seen in decisions about product design and privacy. Products are often designed not just to serve their main function, but also to gather valuable data along the way. The trick is to find opportunities to tweak your product or service to improve the data you collect.

Take Spotify as an example. They have a heap of data generated from a single service—music streaming—which they then use for a totally different, but highly profitable, goal—advertising. This shows how existing data can be repurposed for something else to generate a ton of revenue.

The digital world is loaded with examples like this. Spotify uses listening data for ad targeting, Uber uses ride data for city planning recommendations, Duolingo uses language learning data to improve machine learning for translation, and online educational platforms could potentially use course completion data to promote relevant future courses. The common theme here is a system originally designed for one purpose, but for which, the extra data gathered can be used for other things.

However, it's crucial to tread this path carefully, always being aware of privacy regulations and other restrictions. The challenge isn't just about gathering data but figuring out how to creatively and responsibly use it to inform product decisions. This could involve selling the data or using it to improve your own product or service—like optimizing the placement of ads based on listening habits.

The job now is to carefully examine your data collection practices and figure out how you can profit from the existing data. Unearthing this hidden treasure could unlock potential you never knew existed, paving the way for new opportunities for growth and innovation.

Combining Data for Deeper Insights

Boosting Value by Bridging Data

The power of data grows massively when we move past the idea of looking at each dataset on its own. Usually, the real magic pops up when we bring together datasets from different places. This approach can create something that's worth way more than the sum of its separate parts. However, this process comes with its own unique challenges, especially when it's about bringing together datasets with different structures, legal implications, and financial consequences.

Let's crack open a common problem that often pops up in the process of merging datasets. Let's say you have two datasets, A and B, which come from two different places, and you want to combine them. One problem you might bump into is the lack of common identifiers. For example, merging two datasets based on *username* and *e-mail* might not be enough to create a unique identifier. Despite these possible roadblocks, getting past them can unlock a ton of value.

Take, for example, the challenge of predicting movie box office success. This is a high-stakes problem, as effective marketing strategies can be planned once movies with the potential for big success are identified. The solution to this problem can be found in the data repositories of various places. Movie review aggregators like IMDb and Rotten Tomatoes have heaps of information about movies' ratings. However, the actual box office numbers that track the movies which are big hits are kept by the movie studios themselves.

Now, imagine a situation where we could bring together these datasets—the movie studio's box office data (B) and IMDb's rating data (A)—to predict a movie's likelihood of being a big hit and then plan smart marketing campaigns. IMDb turned this idea into reality by forming data alliances with several movie studios, merging their data with the studios' box office records, and in doing so, uncovering valuable insights.

Pondering the Blend of Datasets

When contemplating merging datasets, a few key questions pop up. First, how tough is the task? Are there financial implications, legal hurdles, or practical difficulties related to the process? Second, what's the value proposition? What will the resulting terrain be once the datasets are put together, and how beneficial would that be?

A perfect example of such a successful data combination can be seen in the concept of *consumer behavior profiling*. This involves merging data from e-commerce platforms like Amazon with browsing histories from companies like Google. The result? Enhanced customer preference profiles that help businesses tailor their offerings, thus improving customer satisfaction and boosting sales.

Essentially, the act of merging data can dig up massive value. While legal, financial, and operational obstacles may surface, the potential rewards often surpass these challenges. Therefore, if you're the holder of a dataset, it could be valuable to look for possible partners with data that enhances yours. This mutual merger might let you forecast previously elusive outcomes, thereby extracting huge value from the process and revealing paths to new insights and opportunities.

Selling Infrastructure

Supplying Tools

Our third pillar of exploration revolves around the notion of *supplying the treasure hunters*. This concept echoes the era of the Gold Rush in the 1800s. Amid the frenzied hunt for gold, there was a significant demand for equipment like metal detectors and gold pans. Not everyone had the inclination or means to create their own tools, so they opted to buy them instead. If we relate this concept to the realm of AI and machine learning, it evolves into providing those golden instruments that empower businesses to explore and extract value from their data.

Consider a local chain of coffee shops, *Daily Brew*, and their decisions on what coffee blends to offer. In their Seattle branches, you might find a larger selection of dark roasts compared to the lighter roasts popular in their Miami outlets. Such inventory decisions demand an ongoing stream of data about customer preferences across various locations, not just from their own outlets but also from competing brands.

However, this data treasure chest could pose a challenge for *Daily Brew*. This is where firms like *MarketLens* step in. They're the modern-day equipment suppliers, providing analytics services to collect information about the variety of coffee blends and related products that companies nationwide are selling. They consolidate this data and provide it to businesses. This invaluable service enables businesses to make data-driven decisions about what coffee blends to offer.

The key insight here revolves around cost arbitrage. It may be expensive for one company to gather all this data, but it becomes a treasure trove if one organization collects all the data and distributes it among many. In this case, *MarketLens* exemplifies the *supplying the treasure hunters* strategy.

Companies across various industries are leveraging this opportunity. For instance, consider *PhysioNet*, a platform devoted to preserving physiological datasets. They generate revenue by selling this data to interested parties. Then there's *PropertyRadar*, collecting data related to the real estate market and selling it to the top bidder. For a single property management company, the cost of independently collecting data might be hard to justify. However, procuring it from a third party like *PropertyRadar* could be a strategic move.

So, keep an eye out for those opportunities where the demand for data is distributed across many, but the individual cost of collection could be prohibitive. This could be your golden opportunity to step in and provide those essential *treasure hunting tools*, enabling businesses to strike it rich in their data-laden mines.

Levi Strauss

During the crazy times of the California Gold Rush, a savvy businessman named Levi Strauss decided to try his luck in the rapidly growing city of San Francisco. He set up a dry goods store to serve the flood of people who were rushing in, lured by the promise of gold. But for Strauss, it wasn't enough to just go along with what was already happening. He paid close attention to the unique needs of his new neighbors, especially the miners who were working their fingers to the bone.

Spotting their desperate need for tough clothing that could take a beating, Strauss joined forces with Jacob Davis, a superskilled tailor, to come up with a game-changing solution in workwear design. In 1873, they patented their brainchild: work pants strengthened with solid copper rivets, which the world now knows as blue jeans. The release of these tough-as-nails pants, complete with strengthened pockets and durable rivets, provided a revolutionary option for miners and workers who were tired of their work clothes falling apart.

News of Levi Strauss's kick-ass jeans spread like wildfire through the mining communities, crossing borders and reaching workers in various industries. Everyone was buzzing about these innovative pants, praising their unbeatable comfort and lasting durability. Demand went through the roof, pushing their popularity way beyond Strauss's original customer base of San Francisco miners.

This spike in demand marked the birth of the iconic Levi's denim brand, a simple idea that grew into a global phenomenon. Today, it's a timeless symbol of American culture. Its roots in the Gold Rush serve as a reminder of the power of careful observation, targeted innovation, and the ability to tap into the hidden potential of existing resources. Whether you're mining for gold or mining for data, this historical tale highlights the importance of tailoring your business strategy to meet the unserved needs of a particular group of people. By doing this, you can create lasting value and leave a legacy that stands the test of time.

Wells Fargo

Back in the mid-19th century, in the middle of the Gold Rush, two smart guys named Henry Wells and William Fargo spotted a need that everyone else was overlooking in the mad dash for gold. They saw that the booming communities in California, all sparked by the Gold Rush, were crying out for secure transport and financial services that just weren't available at the time.

In 1852, they decided to cash in on this opportunity by setting up Wells Fargo & Company. Their goal was to fill this massive gap in the market and offer much-needed services to the thriving communities. At first, the company concentrated on express delivery, but they quickly became the go-to for individuals and businesses who needed to move valuable goods around. Wells Fargo was the safe and reliable way for miners to send their precious gold dust back to their homes or banks.

Wells Fargo's business depended on a wide network of stagecoach routes, strategically placed express offices in key locations, and extremely secure vaults in which miners could trust their hard-earned gold was safe. In a time marked by unpredictability and risk-taking, the dependability and safety offered by Wells Fargo was like a calming presence—something that was worth its weight in gold in such unstable times.

As the company built up its reputation and won the trust of the communities it served, Wells Fargo started to broaden its range of services. They added banking facilities, money transfer services, and even telegraphic communications to their offerings. They did all this with a constant focus on security, reliability, and efficient operations—things that really struck a chord with their customers.

Throughout the Gold Rush and beyond, Wells Fargo's growth played a key role in boosting trade and commerce. The company seized the opportunity presented by the Gold Rush, but not by joining the chaotic scramble for gold. Instead, they focused on addressing the needs that sprang from it. This story of Wells Fargo is a powerful lesson in spotting gaps in the market, grabbing them, and continually innovating to meet the ever-changing needs of your customers.

Nvidia in the New Gold Rush

In today's fast-paced tech world, we're seeing a new kind of gold rush—one that's powered by the endless possibilities of AI that can create new stuff (generative AI). Just as the miners in the California Gold Rush needed the right gear to find gold, today's AI explorers need the right tools and setup to unlock all the cool things that generative AI can do. Nvidia, a leading company in cutting-edge tech, saw this growing need and smartly positioned itself as the go-to provider of the essential *picks and shovels* for the AI gold rush.

Just as folks like Levi Strauss and Wells Fargo cleverly cashed in on the Gold Rush by supplying much-needed tools to the miners, Nvidia did the same in the digital era. They didn't just sit on the sidelines. They grabbed the chance to be a key player in supporting the growing community of AI researchers, developers, and fans.

Nvidia provided essential hardware and software tools to these AI practitioners, making itself an integral part of the AI ecosystem. But they didn't stop at just supplying the hardware. They knew that the expanding field of AI came with its own set of tricky challenges. So, Nvidia also supplied software development kits and platforms like CUDA for parallel computing, which made programming their GPUs for AI tasks a lot easier.

Nvidia's smart positioning shows how important it is to understand how new industries work and what specific demands they bring. By giving AI enthusiasts the tools and tech they needed, Nvidia became more than just a supplier; it became a key partner in the search for ground-breaking developments in generative AI. Basically, Nvidia is a shining example of a company that understands the value of giving others the tools they need to unlock the potential of a new frontier—just like the guys who supplied picks and shovels during the Gold Rush. Their approach shows how rewarding it can be when you spot and meet the crucial needs of an up-and-coming industry.

The Lens of Innovation

Learning From Others

Some Inspiration From Success Stories

Pivoting from our previous talks about tasks and data, we're now going to focus on the fun stuff: innovation itself. Here's a question that might pop up: how are folks applying machine learning in the real world? What success stories can we learn from, and how can we use those strategies to create our own path?

There's nothing wrong with borrowing ideas, especially when it comes to AI. Think about ongoing research where tech and cardiology meet. The goal here is to use machine learning to read ECGs and ultrasound images, which could shake things up for the better. While doing this kind of research might seem out of reach for us, the important point is that AI is getting really good at recognizing images.

This idea kicked off with large-scale image recognition competitions. Around 2015, machine learning started to beat humans at this task. The possible uses of this improved skill are wonderfully exciting. Consider textile factories, where cloth is currently inspected for defects by workers. Why not automate this job, using machine learning to spot problems?

Or let's think about the farming industry. Given that machines can *see* as well as humans, how can we apply this in farming? The opportunities for change are huge, with each implementation being tweaked to meet the unique needs and challenges of a particular industry.

The key thing to learn from these examples is that machines are getting really good at doing complex tasks that, until recently, were mostly done by people. Our job—and also our opportunity—is to find new uses where these advances can do the most good.

There have been really cool recent development is in language processing. Machines are getting better and better at understanding and working with language. We see this every day, in the predictive text and automated responses we use in our chats and e-mails. The big question is, how can we use this growing ability in new ways?

Looking at past successes can show us the potential in these new capabilities. By deliberately adopting this innovation-focused mindset, we can spot chances to use these technologies in new and exciting ways. This is what *borrowing* is all about in AI innovation. With this in mind, let's keep exploring and move on to the next rule.

Demystify Value

Navigating the Hype to Create Real-World Value

In the fast and ever-evolving world of AI, it's critical to distinguish between buzz and real opportunities. In this section, we'll see how to concentrate on the practical aspects of AI, and tune out the noise that often accompanies overblown claims.

Sometimes, the appeal of future promises can make us undervalue the might and potential of what's right in front of us. Consider the constant hype around completely automated drones, for instance. We're perpetually told they're *just around the corner*. But while these grand visions haven't fully materialized yet, a more grounded view prompts us to ask: how can we create a simpler version that works and is handy today?

Our ideas for automated drones are definitely big, but the practical obstacles—from societal and technological to legal—are massive. While we're waiting, what can we conceive and actualize as simpler versions of this tech?

One neat example is the use of small, automated drones to deliver books within libraries. This applies machine learning in a relatively controlled environment, where speeds are low and navigation is less unpredictable. Initial programs have shown promising results in this area.

Shifting to warehouse management, automated tech can help move boxes from one part of the warehouse to another. It might not be flying through the open air, but in a controlled environment, it's an ideal use of machine learning. The task is specific: moving goods around, not flying over a city.

Or consider the automated lawn mower, an autonomous gardening tool. The job it performs in planning a route and navigating around a garden is somewhat similar to what we want from an automated drone, just on a smaller, more manageable scale.

These simpler uses might lack the glamor or thrill of their fully developed counterparts, but they still pack a lot of value. And the cool thing is that they don't require you to be at the absolute forefront of tech. Instead, you take the most ambitious current version of the innovation and brainstorm a more achievable, simplified version.

A recent instance is the hype around AI chatbots. The concept of fully autonomous conversational AI is indeed fascinating, but the real value lies in more modest uses. An AI customer service assistant is a good example. It might not replace human customer service reps, but it can help answer frequently asked questions and guide users through a website. Or consider a model that sends out automated reminder e-mails—it might not be a chatbot capable of engaging in fully human-like conversations, but it's handy and offers valuable assistance.

The central idea behind the *demystifying value* approach is straightforward: identify the overhyped potential future use and develop a simpler, more practical version that offers genuine value now. It might not grab the same kind of headlines, but it is a reliable way to create valuable solutions while we're waiting for our bigger dreams to come to life.

The Lens of Product

The Magic of Making Things Smart

Before we move onto our last guiding principle, let's pause for a moment to look back at the strategies we've already gone through. We started with strategies that focused on tasks, pointing out tasks that could be made better by automating or adding predictive elements. After that, we looked at strategies based on data, examining how to use existing data, combine data from different sources, or even create infrastructure that others need—basically providing the *picks and shovels* for our time. After that, we moved into strategies driven by innovation, looking at existing uses of AI and machine learning, and thinking about how we could borrow and apply these ideas to new contexts or strip away the hype around certain AI uses to find practical, applicable uses.

Now, we're moving to our final set of strategies, which are all about the production process. The big question here is, how can we make the ways we produce goods, provide services, and do various tasks better and more streamlined?

The first golden rule in this final topic is the concept of making something *smart*. Picture a smart alarm clock that learns your sleeping patterns and adjusts your wake-up times accordingly. But why would this be handy? To shed some light on this, let's mull over a seemingly unrelated but insightful application.

If you hang out in any online music community, you're likely to see lots of folks strumming guitars with incorrect technique, which can lead to ineffective practice or, worse, repetitive strain injuries. A professional music teacher could surely guide and correct these individuals—but could we make this process *smart*?

How could we apply our *make something smart* golden rule in this scenario? How could we make a guitar stand or music practice smart?

One possible answer could be to mount a camera on the guitar stand to observe people's hand positions and provide instant feedback. Are they holding the chords right? Is their strumming technique correct? What specific song are they trying to play? A product like RiffMaster, which employs machine learning for these purposes, offers an encouraging solution. It identifies your hand movements in three dimensions and adds valuable insights on top of this understanding.

In this manner, making something smart not only enhances the process but also ensures accuracy and safety, offering a fresh take on a time-honored practice. The emergence of AI and machine learning enables us to view traditional processes in a new light, unveiling numerous opportunities for innovation and enhancement.

Infusing *Smartness* Into Everyday Life

This rule is a fantastic method to kickstart the imagination. It's all about grabbing ordinary items or regular tasks and spicing them up with a little bit of AI. Let's get into some examples to illustrate what I'm talking about.

Think about doors. When there's a rush at a shopping mall or a cinema, you often see security personnel manually opening and closing doors—something usually done automatically. Why do they do that? Well, it's because humans can respond faster to changes in crowd flow than an automated system can. They can manage a bunch of people coming from one direction and none from another, opening and closing the doors as needed. We can't have security staff doing this all the time because it'd be way too expensive. But what if we could give doors a mind of their own?

Imagine doors with top-notch sensors and cameras, much better than the basic ones we have now that can only detect if a person is there or not. These *smart* doors could learn to see crowds coming from a distance and adjust the opening and closing to reduce congestion. Sure, safety is paramount here, and any mishaps could cause accidents. But, isn't it a cool concept to use AI to make doors smarter? It's kind of hard to believe that 20 years from now, we'll still be pushing a door with a *Pull* sign on it.

Let's change lanes and think about something you use every day—your shoes. Now, you might be questioning, "how on earth can AI fit into this scenario?" Well, there's a burgeoning interest in making our walking routines smarter. With AI, your shoes could analyze your stride to spot signs of potential foot problems or changes in your gait. This might sound a bit peculiar, but considerable resources are being invested in this area because there's a belief that our walking patterns could give us important insights about our physical health in the future.

The scope of this *making something smart* principle is truly vast. Imagine a smart umbrella that not only alerts you when it's about to rain but also gives you advice, linking the forecast to things like your overall health and whether you should go for that jog or not.

This rule nudges us to see *smartness* all around, to peek beyond what's immediately visible. Take a common object or a routine task and ponder how you could make it smarter with AI. What data could you extract from it? What could you forecast using that data? By posing these questions and thinking outside the box, we can make our world a more efficient, responsive, and intelligent place.

Find a Production Pain Point

A Solution to Production Roadblocks

Another crucial area is one we can label as *tackling manufacturing glitches*. It's all about identifying and handling issues that obstruct the seamless production of goods, which could be eating into valuable time and resources.

Many industries and manufacturing units face these types of challenges. It could be a software glitch or a malfunctioning piece of equipment. Whenever these issues crop up and work comes to a standstill, the financial toll can be substantial. These unforeseen setbacks can significantly impact an organization's bottom line. So, how do AI and machine learning fit into this scenario? It boils down to their potential to foresee problems before they occur.

Consider the automobile industry as an example. If a car production line halts due to a machine failure, the costs can be astronomical, not just in monetary terms but also considering production delays. Currently, the primary strategies to tackle this are hoping that nothing goes wrong, managing downtime and repair expenses when things do go haywire, or conducting checks on all machinery after each production cycle. While it's critical to inspect all essential parts, it's also an incredibly time-consuming and costly procedure.

This is where AI and machine learning could provide a novel approach. The significant point here is that you can often foresee a malfunction. Before a machine grinds to a halt entirely, it usually exhibits certain symptoms. If we monitor these signs, we can probably predict if a component is about to malfunction.

Consider a machine that begins to vibrate slightly, then increasingly so, or produces unusual sounds, or overheats. These are all red flags that something might be on the brink of failure. They don't always imply that a complete breakdown is imminent, but they do offer us a chance to intervene before it occurs.

This approach is commonly referred to as predictive maintenance. Instead of shutting down a production line immediately due to an issue, predictive maintenance enables us to anticipate repairs before they become necessary. If we know a particular part is likely to fail in three days, we have time to arrange the repair during a lull period or source the replacement parts we need, which aids in cost management and minimizes downtime.

Employing AI and machine learning for this purpose means we can utilize data to spot anomalies or unusual occurrences that might signal impending equipment failure. By examining these patterns, we can anticipate when a machine is prone to malfunction and prepare accordingly. This proactive approach to managing manufacturing glitches would provide industries with a more efficient and cost-effective solution, allowing them to circumvent problems before they arise and maintain a smooth operation.

Diverse Applications of Failure Prediction

The concept of identifying early indications of failure can significantly enhance efficiency. And this doesn't just apply to machinery. This notion of *predictive upkeep*—intervening promptly before minor issues morph into major problems—can be employed across a vast spectrum of domains, from maintaining employee productivity to ensuring software security. This kind of foresight could allow us to preempt failures before they transpire.

Let's imagine you're managing a power plant. You might employ sensor data, such as pressure, humidity, or electricity consumption as your X variables in your predictive model. If these start behaving oddly, it could indicate a component is nearing a breakdown. Thus, you can proactively undertake maintenance, repair the component, or replace it with a new one. This way, you maintain a smoothly functioning operation with minimal downtime.

However, this kind of strategy isn't confined to machinery. It can also prove exceptionally useful in areas like human resources. A company might monitor employees' performance metrics or feedback surveys as vital X variables. By analyzing trends in these metrics, it might be able to predict job satisfaction trends or anticipate if it's about to face a mass exodus of talent. If there's a decline in job satisfaction, the company can act swiftly by addressing grievances, modifying its human resources (HR) policies, or altering its work culture. This way, it would avoid damaging employee morale and losing valuable talent.

The same applies to software security. By examining patterns in system logs, cybersecurity teams might be able to predict an imminent cyberattack. If they foresee this, they can step in early by patching vulnerabilities, bolstering firewalls, or increasing surveillance to prevent a breach.

In all these scenarios, we're utilizing predictive analysis to anticipate an adverse outcome and implementing preventive measures based on what we see. An intriguing aspect of this is that, if our preventive action is successful, it alters the future data that our model was predicting. For instance, if a model predicts a security breach and the cybersecurity team intervenes effectively, the breach doesn't occur. Hence, the model's prediction didn't materialize. This *contamination* of data might complicate training future machine learning models because our actions have changed the anticipated outcome.

This illustrates how vital it is to design AI and machine learning models that can account for these kinds of interventions and adjust their predictions accordingly. By doing this, we can continually enhance the precision and effectiveness of our models, enabling us to stay ahead of potential issues in a multitude of domains.

Predictive Models in Action

Predictive models, like the ones we've discussed, can be real game-changers. Still, they've got their own set of headaches. But hey, with the right game plan and actions, we can conquer these challenges and end up with models that truly pack a punch.

One big speed bump is the need for randomized controls or holdout samples. That's when we keep a chunk of data where we don't act on the predictions at all. This gives us a clean set of data where the things we predicted can unfold without us stepping in. It's a good way to see if our model's hitting the bullseye. But it can also whip up some ethical dilemmas, especially in areas like predicting when an employee might quit or when a company might be on the verge of a cyberattack.

Let's imagine we're predicting cyberattacks based on previous system weaknesses. If we see an attack coming, we can beef up our security to fend it off. But then, there's this ethical question: should we hold back and not take action over a sample batch of systems predicted to be at risk?

Predictive models can also be handy for stuff like investing in stocks, predicting whether a stock's value will tank based on past performance and market trends. Here, the action could be to sell off the stock or maybe even decide not to invest in the first place. Again, we run into an ethical question: should we sit back and not take action with a group of stocks likely to nose-dive?

In all these situations, we're trying to predict a bad outcome (the *problem*) using the data we have. The aim is to put the brakes on or ameliorate the bad outcome with specific actions. We're seeing heaps of AI and machine learning systems being built and used for these purposes. It's a big task, but man, it's also pretty rewarding.

The main thing to keep in mind is that getting predictions spot-on is crucial, but we also need to think hard about how we act based on those predictions. We've got to consider the ethics, strike a balance between keeping our data clean and stepping in when needed, and keep updating our model based on what we see. By doing this, we can use these predictive techniques to dial down or avoid bad outcomes in all sorts of situations.

Seeing the Predictable in the Unpredictable

The key idea here is all about noticing *costly events*—those things that go wrong or cause harm—and wondering if we could see them coming. If we had some warning about these things, could we change the way we act? If the answer is yes, then it's worth trying to predict these events and change our behavior ahead of time.

One reason we might not do this is that we assume these things can't be predicted. We might not see these unwanted events as being predictable. For instance, you might not hear about a complaint made against a police officer and immediately think, "I could've predicted that." But actually, a lot of these incidents can be predicted. Information from colleagues, administrative records, past interactions, and historical complaints are just some of the data that could help us see these things coming.

We need to shift our thinking and understand that a lot of the things we think are unpredictable can actually be predicted if we approach them with the right tools and mindset.

Another reason we might miss these opportunities is that we don't collect the right information to make predictions. To predict when equipment might fail, for example, we need sensors on the machines to gather data on things like vibrations. If we don't set up a system to collect this data from the start, we won't be able to see the potential predictability of the failure. Our ability to deal with production bottlenecks could be hampered by not gathering the right data.

The big point to remember here is the importance of collecting data proactively. Even if some information doesn't seem useful right away, it could become really important for future predictions. It might be worth our while to go the extra mile and set up sensors and data collection systems. The data we collect might show us that the failures we're worried about aren't random, but things we can predict.

The Pareto Principle

Putting the Pareto Principle to Work

The Pareto principle, or what many call the 80/20 rule, says that a handful of causes lead to the lion's share of effects in loads of areas, including business and, yes, AI. You can spot this rule in action just about everywhere.

Think about a coffee shop. What chunk of customer orders could be met with a standard set of drink preparations? Given that coffee shops usually have a set menu and customers mostly order from that, the chances are a big part of the orders can be managed with a few standard recipes. There you have it, the Pareto principle at work. A small set of recipes covers most customer orders.

Let's dig a bit deeper with an example closer to AI: an automated coffee machine. Picture three customers, each with different orders of varying customization and complexity. Every order is unique, with customers choosing their unique blends. However, the automated machine responds the same way to all three, asking for the payment before preparing the order.

This example captures the heart of the Pareto principle: a small number of settings and modes effectively handling most customer orders. But keep in mind, while a hefty chunk of service can be sorted using preset modes, there will always be orders that throw us a curveball.

Imagine a fourth customer with a wacky request—they want a coffee blend that isn't on the menu. This order doesn't neatly fit into a preset mode. It calls for human action, pointing out an important fact; while automation is a whiz at taking care of most routine tasks, there's always a "long tail" of out-of-the-ordinary cases that need the flexibility and understanding that only humans can provide.

So, the Pareto principle highlights the need to concentrate on automating certain tasks, instead of trying to automate a whole job. Automation and AI can pick up the slack for the repetitive and high-volume tasks, while humans tackle the complex, unexpected, and subtle cases, showing the awesome teamwork of human and AI.

The Pareto principle is a handy guide for finding the areas where automation can make the most impact, but it's got its limits: the long tail of events that don't quite fit under our range of preset modes. Balancing automation and human interaction to deal with these special cases is the key to keeping a system nimble and effective.

Crafting Strategy With the Pareto Principle and AI Triage

The main takeaway from using the Pareto principle in AI is that, while we might not be able to automate everything, we can take care of a good chunk of the simpler tasks. This can seriously boost how much we can get done and how efficiently we do it. The key idea here is understanding that not every job can or should be automated. However, a hefty chunk of them can be automated, leading to big improvements.

This point gets us to a vital part of AI strategy: AI triage. In this approach, AI takes on most of the routine tasks, leaving the trickier or unexpected ones for humans to deal with. It's like a great tag-team effort between artificial and human smarts, whereby AI tackles the boring, predictable work, and humans sort out the rest, making the best use of both.

One of the main challenges with this approach is figuring out how to spot and send the more complex cases to human agents without messing up the customer's experience. The way we set up this environment can make a big difference in how well it works.

We can think about a few possible setups. The simplest one might be a system where every chat starts with an AI chatbot. The AI keeps the chat going until the customer asks to speak with a human or the chat starts to go off-track or goes haywire. At this point, the chat gets rerouted to a human agent. This setup puts AI in the driver's seat, calling in human help only when needed.

Another setup might involve a human agent who is always ready to step in, checking and okaying, tweaking, or even completely redoing AI-generated responses as required. In this case, the AI acts as a first shot at a response, with a human in the loop making sure the quality is up to scratch and dealing with more complex chats.

These are just a couple of ways AI can be used in a triage role, using its strengths in dealing with repetitive, high-volume tasks while keeping the human touch where it's most needed. We'll dive deeper into the ins and outs of AI environments and how to design them best in future discussions. For now, though, it's vital to see the game-changing potential AI has in reshaping how work is done, increasing productivity, and improving customer experiences, even when total automation isn't the goal.

Unfolding the Pareto Principle in AI Applications

The 80/20 rule is a really useful lens that we can use to understand how AI operates in all sorts of situations, helping us shape and finetune our AI strategies.

Take the world of tech support, for example. The majority of support requests usually fit into a few common categories. So, wouldn't it be smart to let a chatbot take care of these routine issues? That's exactly what some savvy tech companies do. They deploy chatbots to handle most of these familiar requests, based on their experience with what customers usually need help with. This leaves the human tech support team free to deal with the more complex, oddball problems. It's all about letting AI tackle the regular stuff and letting humans deal with the unique, one-of-a-kind cases.

The same idea works well in areas like automated captioning and voice recognition. When we speak, we often use a bunch of common words again and again. AI is pretty nifty at spotting and transcribing these words. Sure, it might have a tough time with unusual slang or specialized jargon, but it handles the everyday language like a champ. And that's what counts most of the time.

But it's not just about simple tasks like voice recognition and tech support queries. This principle is at play even in high-tech systems like an AI restaurant table booking service. You might think making a reservation could lead to all sorts of different chats, right? But in reality, most of these conversations stick to a few main details—how many diners, what date and time, and any specific seating needs. The AI booking service might trip up with more rare requests, but it nails it for the majority of standard reservations.

So what's the key lesson here? The Pareto principle is like a secret superpower for AI. It tells us that we can achieve a lot by zooming in on a small set of common patterns and leaving the unique, out-of-the-ordinary stuff to humans. It's like a global positioning system (GPS) guiding us along the quickest route to automating the things that really matter. This helps us decide where to point our AI efforts, making our AI tools more efficient and helping them excel at what they do best.

The Impact on AI

The point we're discussing in this section is like a secret sauce that's added to various aspects of life and fields of study. It tells us that a tiny bit of something can often lead to a whole lot of something else. And although it sounds simple, this principle packs a punch when it comes to shaping the ways we use AI.

One of the main hurdles we face with perfecting AI is dealing with the *long tail*, or the rare or unique situations that don't happen very often. This is one of the reasons why we don't see self-driving cars everywhere yet. Sure, the AI that drives these cars can handle normal driving scenarios and most highways. But when it comes to driving, we need super high levels of accuracy because safety is at stake. The tricky part is coming up with a smooth system that lets a human driver take over when the AI encounters a strange or dangerous situation it can't handle. And let's face it, reaching 100 percent perfection is pretty much impossible, given all the different driving conditions and potential emergency situations that could pop up in the long tail.

So, given this reality, it makes more sense to look for places where we can use AI, even if it's not 100 percent perfect. In other words, we need to find situations where an 80 or 90 percent success rate is good enough.

There are two main things to consider in this quest. First, we have to look at the cost of errors. In some cases, like self-driving cars, the cost of mistakes is high because it can lead to damage to people and property. But in other cases, like AI chatbots in customer service, the cost of mistakes is lower because incorrect answers can be fixed without causing major problems.

The second thing we need to consider is how we handle errors when they happen. The key question is whether there's a practical way to pass these errors to a human or another system. Can the system smoothly switch from AI to human control when things go wrong? Or does the whole system crash and burn, leading to disaster in the 20 percent of cases where the AI messes up?

Figuring out these tricky issues is at the heart of using the Pareto principle for developing AI applications. By finding uses where near-perfect (but not totally perfect) accuracy is okay, and where there are ways to manage errors, we can create AI systems that are both effective and realistic.

Change the Workflow

Lessons From the Horse Carriage and Automobile

Finally, let's chat about the idea of changing the way we do things, or in more formal terms, *workflow transformation*. To make this clearer, let's hop into a time machine and revisit a significant period in history, specifically to the transition from horse carriages to automobiles.

In the old days, the horse carriage was the main mode of transport. It was like the hero of the journey, driving people and goods from Point A to Point B. The entire journey was planned around the capabilities of the horse and carriage. The horse's strength determined the load it could carry, and its endurance dictated how far and how long the journey could be.

This setup meant travel routes and schedules had to be designed a certain way. As the horse's energy was finite and needed replenishing (through rest and feeding), inns and stables were strategically placed along popular routes for necessary stopovers.

But when the automobile rolled onto the scene, everything shifted gears. Cars, powered by combustion engines, could carry heavier loads and travel farther and faster without the need for prolonged rests. This meant that there was no longer a need for frequent stopovers, allowing for more direct routes and flexible travel times. Fuel could be carried onboard and refilled at infrequent intervals, giving much more freedom in planning journeys.

The impact of this change was massive. To truly harness the benefits of automobiles, travel plans had to be significantly reimagined. The transformation wasn't just about switching the horse for an engine-powered vehicle. The real advantage materialized when travel routes, schedules, and logistics were reshaped to align with the capabilities of the automobile.

This historical transition is a great analogy for the transition to AI. We can't just toss AI into a system and expect monumental improvements. Just like the switch from horse carriages to cars, AI can revamp things, but only if we tweak our workflows to accommodate it. This might mean that we need to rearrange our surroundings, rules, and systems to mesh better with AI, letting us unlock all the benefits it can provide.

So, progressing toward an AI future means we have to seriously examine the ways we currently operate. We have to be prepared to make substantial changes to craft a space that's conducive to AI, ensuring we're squeezing out all the possible advantages. This will definitely involve meticulous planning, experimentation, and continuous learning, as we refine the ways that AI fits into our workflows.

From *Stockpiling* to *On-Demand*

Traditionally, manufacturing has been all about the *stockpiling* approach. Basically, manufacturers try to guess what customers will want, make a bunch of products based on those guesses, distribute the products, and then hope their guesses were right. It's a bit like trying to hit a target blindfolded.

While this stockpiling model has been around for ages, it does have its problems. It risks the manufacturer making too much or not enough.

If manufacturers make more than what's needed, they end up with a surplus of unsold goods. Picture parking lots filled with hundreds or even thousands of unsold cars because the manufacturer didn't accurately predict the demand or made too many of a certain model for a certain location. This kind of mistake can lead to too much stock, high storage costs, and potentially waste if the products can spoil or become outdated.

On the flip side, if manufacturers don't make enough, they could be left with not enough stock to meet customer needs. This situation can result in missed sales, unhappy customers, and potentially a loss of market share.

To counter the problems of the stockpiling model, industry is starting to shift toward an *on-demand* approach. This method is about making goods only when they're needed, which can significantly cut the costs of maintaining large inventories. The aim of on-demand manufacturing is to be more efficient, cut down on waste, and be more responsive to what the market wants.

However, the on-demand model comes with its own challenges. It needs a strong supply chain that can quickly adapt to changes in demand. Any disruptions in the supply chain could lead to shortages and hold up production, which can negatively affect customer satisfaction. It also requires sophisticated tools to predict demand to make sure production matches customer needs.

So, manufacturers are left with a tricky question: should they dive into the complex world of on-demand manufacturing? This is where AI could be a game-changer. By using AI for accurate demand prediction, smart supply chain management, and efficient production processes, manufacturers could successfully move from a stockpiling model to an on-demand one. But, just like when we switched from steam power to electricity, this change will mean rethinking current workflows and production processes to make them AI-friendly.

The Conductor in the Orchestra of On-Demand Manufacturing

AI, with its ability to predict and streamline, could potentially revolutionize on-demand manufacturing processes. But there is a big *but* here; how effective it can be depends on how ready you are to rethink your production strategy. If your manufacturing process is still stuck in the stockpiling mindset, the benefits you can get from AI may be limited.

Let's unpack this a bit. At its heart, on-demand manufacturing works like a well-oiled machine. Every part of the supply chain, from getting raw materials to delivering the finished product, works together seamlessly. It's a constant balancing act between having just enough inventory to meet immediate demand and avoiding making too much or not using resources efficiently.

This is where AI can really shine. It can predict customer demand in detail, estimate lead times, find potential bottlenecks in the production process, and optimize how resources are used. With AI, you can make accurate forecasts, which lets you manufacture products *on-demand* to meet customer needs, ensuring a smooth and efficient supply chain.

But to make full use of AI in this way, you need to shift from a stockpiling to an on-demand manufacturing model. If you're ready to make this big change, the benefits from AI could be game-changing. But this change is more than just adding AI into an existing process. It requires a broader shift in strategy that may at first seem unrelated to AI.

Sometimes, the opportunities to use AI might not be obvious in your current operating environment. They might not seem feasible or even relevant within the current setup. But if you're open to making big changes and reshaping your operational strategy, you can create new opportunities for AI. These new opportunities could bring big benefits that wouldn't have been possible by simply adding AI into an unchanged, traditional production process.

This idea fits in with our earlier discussion about closed and open world problems. On-demand manufacturing is kind of a closed world problem, because it deals with a controlled environment with set parameters and limits. It's also closely linked to operations research, which uses advanced analytical methods to help make better decisions. In this context, AI can be an incredibly powerful tool for improving operational efficiency and boosting productivity.

AI With Semiconductors

One industry that has shown some hesitation in adopting AI, despite the immense potential benefits, is the semiconductor industry. The sophisticated nature of this industry, combined with its distinct challenges, often impedes the seamless integration of AI. Intriguingly, the hurdle is not the human factor, as one might presume, but the existing technological infrastructure and its limitations.

There are multiple obstacles to converting the semiconductor industry into an AI-friendly environment. There are problems like system and data format compatibility, the intricacy of data entry and usage, and inconsistent practices in quality control and coding standards, which all act as considerable deterrents. In many ways, the current system in the semiconductor industry appears ill-adapted for the incorporation of AI technologies. If we were to engineer a semiconductor production system from scratch with the primary objective of AI integration, it would be significantly different.

In a semiconductor system structured around AI, standardized protocols for data collection and reporting would become standard. Efficient methods of sharing data across different companies and transferring chip blueprints from one foundry to another would replace outmoded practices such as manually transferring detailed specifications.

The extraordinary potential of AI in the semiconductor industry remains largely untapped, not due to a deficiency of technological progress, but because of a mismatch with the existing system. Current practices in the semiconductor industry are not designed for AI integration. We lack an infrastructure that gathers clean, representative datasets that can be utilized across different institutions. We grapple with the variety of equipment that produces wafer scans in different formats, rendering an AI system trained on one device ineffective on another. This lack of standardization and data sharing impedes the successful integration of AI into the industry.

So, while the role of AI in the semiconductor industry undoubtedly appears promising, attaining success will necessitate a significant shift in how data is generated and handled. We need to reconfigure our systems and processes with the explicit goal of facilitating the deployment of AI. The amalgamation of AI technology and a newly adapted process could potentially yield substantial benefits.

Nonetheless, such a transformation is not without its challenges. Overhauling the way data is managed within the semiconductor industry is an enormous undertaking, requiring substantial resources, time, and effort. It's crucial to ponder whether such changes are essential for the success of AI and if they're realistically achievable within the specific context of your organization.

Opportunities for integrating AI might not initially seem directly tied to AI. However, under the right conditions and with a readiness to implement broader changes, these adjustments could foster an environment where AI can truly flourish. The advantages of this disruptive technology in the semiconductor industry could be immense, but its success is associated with our readiness to modify and overhaul the existing system.

Key Takeaways

- Start With the Task: Let AI take the burden! If you have duties that are monotonous, data-intensive, or simply impossible for humans, AI could become your go-to solution. Bear in mind, it doesn't have to be all or nothing. AI can either independently resolve closed world problems or cooperate with other strategies to handle open world challenges.
- Data Comes First: Consider AI as the ultimate investigator— it thrives on analyzing data. And the best part? It's becoming more skilled at discerning patterns, even when the data isn't labeled. Remember the 80/20 principle? It's just as relevant to AI—a minor portion of your data could supply the majority of your insights.
- Spurring Innovation: Picture AI as a highly efficient office administrator. It can manage routine tasks and refer complex queries to human specialists. If you're unsure about how to begin with AI, identify areas where achieving accuracy 80 to 90 percent of the time would be a significant victory.
- Transforming Production: AI can do wonders in optimizing production processes, like transitioning from a just-in-case to a just-in-time model. However, it's not as straightforward as installing a new software update. To truly unlock AI's potential, you might need to substantially rearrange your production processes.

Evaluating Machine Learning

Getting better and better at the wrong things.

Real-World Consequences of Machine Learning

When you start practicing AI and machine learning, you're probably backed up by a great team or an expert guide who's really good at putting complex models together. But the tricky part isn't just building the models; it's figuring out how well they're doing their job. You might find yourself asking, "Is the model doing what we want it to do? Are the results what we expected?"

Evaluating machine learning models isn't just a techy job given to your team of engineers. You might think you're done once you've got a few metrics in front of you, but that's just the tip of the iceberg. In this chapter, I want to stress that the real success of a model depends on its impact in the real world, in the field it's designed to work in. It's not just about finding out if one model is better than another, if it's an improvement from your current methods, or even if it's ready to launch. The key thing is understanding the potential impact this model could have in the real world.

In all the talk about machine learning, you've probably heard about tons of metrics for measuring predictions—a bunch of stats that give insight into your model's behavior. You've probably heard terms like *false positive rate*, *false negative rate*, or *AUC score* used to describe the model's performance, giving you a sneak peek of its predictive power.

However, it's really important to look beyond these numbers and focus on what they mean in the real world. The big question is, can we turn these metrics into real, tangible outcomes? Your investors and board members aren't just interested in the model's statistical abilities. They're eager to hear about the major changes the model could bring when it's used in real-life situations. The important questions are: how do we turn predictive power into decision-making power? And how can we show the model's impact beyond just numbers?

In this chapter, we'll dig into the idea of prediction quality, but our main goal is to highlight the quality of the decisions it leads to. We're on a mission to find out how machine learning can help us make smarter, more informed decisions, instead of just making statistically impressive predictions.

Looking at our big picture plan, our main concern lies in those moments when the model's predictions don't match up with our expected results. We're on a journey to understand what these mismatches really mean in the grand scheme of things.

To give you a clear idea of how we evaluate a model, let's take a look at a day in the life of your machine learning engineer or data scientist. They usually start by feeding a dataset into a training algorithm to create a model that can make new predictions.

However, the evaluation process goes a step further. The dataset is divided into two parts: about 70 percent becomes the training set, which is used to train the algorithm and create the model. The remaining 30 percent becomes a reserve or validation set.

The engineer or scientist then feeds this reserve set into the already trained model, which makes its predictions. These predictions are compared to the actual outcomes, also known as the *ground truth*. This step creates a comparison between what actually happened and what the model predicted, giving us a statistical measure of how well the model works.

So, when you hear someone say that their model is 90 percent accurate or something similar, it's important to remember that this claim is about the data that wasn't used during training but came from a reserve set. This is the nuts and bolts of evaluating machine learning models—an important aspect that often gets overlooked.

A Pragmatic Approach to Evaluating Models

As we journey further, a central query arises: How do we accurately compare predictions with actual outcomes? While traditional metrics faithfully assess the quality of predictions, the evaluation method may need refinement once the model is ready to be employed in a specific situation. The primary question in your evaluation process should be, "What action am I ready to undertake based on these predictions?"

Consider scenarios of binary classification where Y can only assume two potential values. Envision employing machine learning for credit risk assessment using customer data. Here, Y = 1 signifies that the customer is a credit risk, while Y = 0 suggests they're not. The evaluation in this context hinges on your intended use of the predictions.

It's crucial to note that even though Y is binary, predictions frequently aren't. Most of the time, models yield a score between 0 and 1, which can be perceived as the probability of a customer being a credit risk. At times, this probability might suffice, but when you need to form firm decisions based on these odds, you might opt for a more simplistic approach.

For instance, you could establish a threshold, say, 0.4, and decide to decline a loan if the model's prediction surpasses this limit. If the prediction falls below this threshold, you might choose to approve the loan. At this juncture, the way you utilize these predictions affects the evaluation of the model.

In this context, two types of mistakes can transpire. These errors can be depicted using a 2 × 2 table, where columns represent the actual outcome (credit risk or not), and rows illustrate the decisions made (loan approved or declined).

There are two instances where our decision aligns with reality: when the customer is not a credit risk and we approve the loan, or when the customer is a credit risk and we decline the loan. However, we must also contemplate two types of errors: false positives and false negatives. A false positive occurs when a customer isn't a credit risk, but we decide to decline the loan. Conversely, a false negative happens when a customer is a credit risk, but we decide to approve the loan.

These errors are not only distinct, but they also bear different consequences. So, when someone claims their model has 90 percent accuracy, a dash of skepticism is necessary. Such an assertion conflates these two error types together, and you might harbor more concern about one type than the other. For example, approving a loan to a credit risk is certainly a graver mistake than declining a loan to a customer who isn't a credit risk.

Our objective is to comprehend these different types of error and the potential impact each one carries. This understanding will aid you in deciding the significance you should accord to each type of error.

The false negative rate and the false positive rate are defined as the fraction of customers who were credit risks but got their loans approved and the fraction of customers who were not credit risks but had their loans declined, respectively. These metrics can prove immensely valuable as they quantify the frequency of your mistakes for each group of customers.

However, these definitions both come under the wider concept of prediction quality, indicating how often predictions are accurate or erroneous.

Many decisions about the use of machine learning revolve around the costs of different error types and strategies to mitigate them. Mistakes are inevitable, but your aim should be to minimize the financial and operational impact of these errors and finetune your model to reduce the more costly ones. Let's examine what this idea entails in real-world scenarios.

Understanding the Tradeoffs

In the sphere of investing, there's an insightful concept known as the *margin of safety*. This idea originates from investment gurus like Benjamin Graham. They advocate the principle that it's preferable to forego multiple good deals than to risk a substantial loss on a bad one. This perspective vividly illustrates the distinct costs associated with false positives and false negatives.

Consider it in this light: bypassing a profitable investment is similar to a false negative—a missed opportunity for financial gain. Conversely, committing to a poor investment mirrors a false positive—mistakenly identifying a losing proposition as profitable. Consequently, Graham's principle of the margin of safety implies that the cost incurred from one false positive (a bad investment) significantly outweighs the cost of numerous false negatives (missed good deals).

Graham's philosophy provides valuable insights into managing errors in the investment sector. If you perceive false positives as particularly detrimental (which they are, given their financial implications), you'd want your investment strategy to minimize these errors, even if that potentially means missing some profitable opportunities.

So, what is the relevance of this to large language models?

Language models, like ChatGPT, commonly predict or generate text, which is subsequently evaluated for its accuracy and usefulness. At this point, you establish a confidence threshold—how confident do you need to be about the validity of the generated text before choosing to display it instead of a neutral *uncertain* response?

For instance, ChatGPT might respond with "Apologies, but this query is too complex for me to provide a definitive answer." What's happening is an assessment of the question's complexity. If the model deems the question as exceeding a certain complexity threshold, it opts to withhold a response. This threshold determination arises from weighing the consequences of false positives and false negatives.

Training these large language models involves two phases. The first phase sees the model consuming vast amounts of Internet text and primarily focusing on predicting the next word instead of performing as a chatbot. The second phase involves acquiring human feedback on diverse questions and responses, emphasizing the quality of the responses. It's during this phase that factors like utility, safety, and accuracy get integrated. For example, statements that are initially factually incorrect may receive high scores. However, as the model aligns more with human preferences, it starts to adjust these scores.

In essence, this scenario showcases a tradeoff inherent not just to machine learning but also to many decision-making processes. If you elevate your thresholds or standards, false positives tend to decrease while false negatives increase. Conversely, lowering your standards generally increases false positives and reduces false negatives. This principle is prevalent in the decision theory, but it's particularly prominent in machine learning.

Adapting Decision Contexts in Machine Learning

Up to now, we have mostly been looking through the lens of the decision makers, like an e-commerce company considering the cost of errors. But it's essential to remember that the folks on the other side—let's say, customers—also have costs to deal with. For example, if an e-commerce site makes a mistake and sends the wrong product, it's the customer who has to deal with the hassle of returning it. And sadly, these types of costs, which impact the customers, are often forgotten by the decision makers.

We tend to zoom in on the costs that the decision maker has to deal with, and that sets a certain boundary for making decisions. But if we considered the costs that both the customer and the e-commerce site have to bear, we might end up choosing a different boundary. Let's not forget, incentives really do guide these decisions.

We see something similar in the entertainment industry. Both the platform (like a streaming service) and the viewer bear costs. When deciding how to set boundaries and what costs to pass on to people, we've got to think about whose interests and costs we're putting first.

When it comes to checking out machine learning models, you'll often run into the rates of false positives and false negatives, and that involves assessing the costs of mistakes. But these costs aren't fixed. They can change based on the rules we set. Let's say we have a model that's designed to predict if a movie will be a hit or a flop based on the trailer. The real costs of making a mistake won't be clear until we've figured out what actions we'll take based on that prediction.

Think about this: a model predicts a movie will be a hit, and based on that prediction, the studio decides to invest in a big marketing campaign. The cost of getting it wrong here is high: a false positive means money is wasted on marketing a flop, while a false negative means a missed opportunity to market a potential hit. Here, we might want to have a balanced threshold. But, if instead of launching a massive campaign, we only decided to adjust the release date based on the prediction, the costs of getting it wrong wouldn't be as heavy. It's the same model and data, but a different action changes how we see the costs of mistakes.

So, instead of just deciding on thresholds, we should think about how we can shape the environment around the model to get better tradeoffs between different types of errors. By using a different action, like adjusting the release date, we could change our chosen thresholds. You get to decide what actions to take based on a model and how to build the environment around it.

Usually, in machine learning and decision theory, we assume that the costs for false positives and false negatives are fixed, and then we just crunch the numbers to get your threshold. But really, we should be thinking about how we can tweak the decision environment to lower the costs of making mistakes.

If the decision-making process forces you to choose between bad and worse errors, it might be a good idea to take a step back and rethink the whole situation. Like a movie studio planning a huge marketing campaign based on a model's predictions might instead consider less expensive actions, or even involve human experts in the decision-making process.

Shifting Focus From Predictions to Decisions

So, we've spent a fair bit of time discussing how we can gauge the quality of our model's predictions. Now, it's time to turn the tables. Instead of zooming in on the accuracy of predictions, let's think about the decisions these predictions enable us to make. After all, it's not just about forecasting rain, but about whether we should carry an umbrella, isn't it?

In this next part of our journey, we're going to find out how to pinpoint and measure the outcomes that truly matter to us. Then it's all about putting these predictions to work and figuring out how they affect the decisions we make.

And while we've been discussing models at length, we certainly can't overlook the building blocks of these models—our data. Just like a great recipe needs top-notch ingredients, a solid model needs quality data. So, we're going to delve into how to scrutinize our data to ensure it's up to par before we even start developing our models.

The big takeaway here is we're not just interested in the predictions our model is making but also whether it helps in making sound decisions. It's not simply about whether our model can pass a hypothetical test, but if it's ready to graduate into the real world.

The binary or yes–no situations are straightforward to evaluate, right? But real-world problems are seldom black and white. So, let's start by brushing up on how we handle these simpler binary cases before we tackle more complex scenarios. Let's shift gears and learn not just to predict, but to decide with confidence.

Binary Predictions to Real-World Decisions

Consider a real-life AI-powered solution known as FluSense. This system is designed to predict the spread of flu-like illnesses based on data inputs, such as the sound of coughs in public spaces. Similar to our previous example, we have two versions of this system to consider. In the first version, FluSense directly alerts the health authorities every time it detects the possibility of a flu outbreak. In the second version, it sends the detection data to a human analyst first, who then confirms whether it is indeed indicative of a flu outbreak before alerting the authorities.

Now, let's start evaluating the first version, where FluSense autonomously alerts health authorities when it detects a potential flu outbreak.

In a situation where there's no flu outbreak and FluSense correctly identifies that, everything runs smoothly. No unnecessary alerts are raised, saving both time and resources.

However, if a flu outbreak is occurring and FluSense fails to detect it, this is a case of false negatives. In such an instance, a health crisis could escalate without any alerts being raised, leading to potentially harmful consequences.

What about false positives, where FluSense predicts a flu outbreak when there's none? In this case, health authorities could end up deploying resources unnecessarily, creating strain and leading to wasted efforts. If false positives persist, over time, it could result in a loss of trust in the system's reliability.

Finally, in the best-case scenario where a flu outbreak is in progress and FluSense correctly detects it, the health authorities get alerted sooner than they might have otherwise, potentially allowing them to respond more rapidly and effectively.

This exercise of identifying the potential impacts of our system lets us understand the possible outcomes of deploying FluSense. The system could potentially raise early alerts about flu outbreaks, accelerating response times. However, it could also result in false alerts leading to a waste of resources and potential erosion of trust in the system. In addition, the system may fail to alert us about some actual outbreaks, another negative outcome. These outcomes are essential to consider before deciding on system deployment.

Model Performance Outcomes

Let's convert those statistical metrics into tangible, real-life changes. After all, if you're a city health official looking to adopt this system, you're not necessarily interested in abstract error rates. Rather, you care about what will tangibly change once the system is deployed.

Consider the threshold set for the alerts. As the one orchestrating the system, you have to decide: do you want the system to alert at the slightest hint of a flu outbreak, or should it hold off until the signs are undeniable? Let's assume for now that you've struck the right balance.

The core question, though, isn't just about the accuracy of FluSense. It's about how this tool will enhance decision making. Instead of just asking, "How good is this model?" we should be asking, "How will this system aid us in making better decisions?"

Being able to articulate the impact of the system in this way allows us to compare it to other potential solutions. For instance, if we consider an altered version of FluSense, where an analyst verifies the alerts before they are sent to the health authorities, we can gauge the potential outcomes.

Take the scenario where there's no flu outbreak and the system correctly identifies that. Great! Business as usual. But what if there's an outbreak and the system doesn't detect it? Well, that's a missed opportunity to intervene and control the spread. What about a false alarm? Instead of causing unnecessary panic, this now just eats up an analyst's time.

And when there is an outbreak and it's correctly identified? Well, the analyst now has a chance to verify this before triggering an alert. But remember, analysts aren't infallible. They might miss some genuine outbreaks or confirm false alarms, which will also affect the system's impact.

Expressing the system's performance in terms of these real-world outcomes allows for clearer comparison with the initial, analyst-free FluSense model. It's a more grounded assessment of the system, which health officials can use to make informed decisions about deployment. Rather than getting caught up in the technicalities of error rates, they can understand the practical consequences: How many outbreaks will be detected early? How many false alarms might there be? What is the cost in analyst time? And, inevitably, how many outbreaks might still be missed? These are the real-world metrics that matter.

The Challenge of Chatbot Behavior

Models like ChatGPT and others pose an interesting case. They generate text rather than delivering yes-or-no answers, making it tricky to definitively judge their outputs as right or wrong. For instance, how do we measure the propensity of a model like ChatGPT to generate inappropriate or harmful content, such as hate speech?

Let's say, you're part of OpenAI's team and you want to ensure your models don't produce offensive content. A logical first step would be identifying certain words that shouldn't be used. You could scour the model's outputs for these words or even implement rules to exclude them entirely. It's a good start, but as anyone who's dabbled with sentiment analysis knows, it's practically impossible to capture all instances of hate speech with a predefined set of rules. Here, you might find yourself stepping into the territory of machine learning again, trying to classify given text as hateful or not.

So, let's imagine you're in the early stages of testing and you're trying to assess the kind of text the model generates. You don't want any hateful content, but how do you measure that effectively? A simplified approach could look something like the following.

First, you create a classifier for hate speech. This is a separate machine learning model whose sole purpose is to identify whether a given text is hateful. Then you expose this classifier to the texts generated by ChatGPT, effectively using a machine learning model to assess another.

Humans also play a vital role in this process. You'd generate a collection of model outputs, ask humans to review them, and rate whether they find them offensive or not. These labels help train your hate speech classifier.

At this point, you've basically built a binary classification problem (is the output hateful, or not?) to evaluate the performance of an open-ended text generation model. Now you can apply similar evaluation techniques to the one that we've used for binary classification problems.

The metrics from this process can tell you how frequently offensive content may pass undetected by your classifier and potentially reach an end-user. This method gives you a tangible way of assessing and refining the behavior of models like ChatGPT.

To recap: We focused on evaluating AI machine learning models and how these models allow for tradeoffs. Sometimes, you might be okay with more false positives, and sometimes, you might be okay with more false negatives. These choices are based on real-world outcomes.

Now, in some cases, these outcomes directly connect to the errors we can observe. But, sometimes, we need to put in a little extra effort to identify and measure these consequences. For instance, with ChatGPT, it's not as simple as saying the answer is right or wrong. There are varying degrees of *bad*, and we have different criteria to evaluate. This requires us to create specific evaluation mechanisms ourselves.

The overall idea is to evaluate your system based on the quality of decisions it enables. Metrics like true positives, false positives, and so on are handy, but they may not be of much use to someone who's deciding whether to deploy this model or not. Our target should be to translate these model metrics into real-world consequences that anyone can understand and engage with. So, the question is, can we contemplate what the consequences of deploying the overall system will be, rather than just relying on metrics that describe model performance?

Evaluating the Data Behind Machine Learning

We're going to assess the data that these machine learning systems are built on and delve into what it really means to have *good data*. How would you identify quality data? And what are the common mistakes people make when they're attempting to curate datasets?

Consider this: a really instructive way to grasp how data collection can falter is to think about product reviews. Consider online shopping platforms that were once plagued with fake reviews, thereby misleading customers and inflating product ratings.

Now, you'd think the primary job of these platforms is to offer accurate product reviews to guide customers, right? It was frustrating for them when they realized their system was flawed and consistently fooled by fake reviews.

This led to a ton of questions and the search for solutions. And the reasons behind these errors, these consistent inaccuracies in reviews, offer great insights into understanding why machine learning models, or the data we assemble for machine learning, can also be faulty. To frame this understanding, I'm going to depict two distinct types of errors.

Firstly, there's the issue of not enough genuine customers writing reviews, people not wanting to share their experiences, and platforms relying too much on easily manipulated rating systems. That's one set of mistakes. The second set includes scenarios where people don't feel comfortable sharing their honest opinions, people changing their reviews, and indecisive people.

I'm going to label these as *labeling errors* and *sampling errors*. Sampling errors are when you pick the wrong people to survey or you've chosen the wrong distribution. Labeling errors come into play when you're trying to assess the sentiments of reviewers. Did you accurately measure their opinions? What mistakes did you make there?

So, there you have it. Two different ways data collection can be flawed. Both are commonly encountered in real life, and we're going to need different strategies to tackle them, or to determine whether we've run into them.

In the world of data collection, labeling errors can often serve as a major stumbling block. In the context of our framework, a labeling error transpires when the data you measure isn't really the data you need. This kind of error crops up frequently, given that there's often a gap between the data we are able to measure and the data we desire to measure. In essence, we often find ourselves measuring proxies for the things we want.

Here's the catch, though: machine learning isn't a magic wand to correct this discrepancy. Contrary to what some might wish, machine learning doesn't predict what we want it to predict, it predicts what we have measured. It's an extremely literal tool, devoid of common sense. If your measurements are incorrect, your predictions will naturally follow suit.

This mismatch between our desired measurements and the actual measurements surfaces quite often, especially on digital platforms. For instance, many online services aspire to gauge their performance based on user satisfaction. However, what they typically end up measuring are user activities, such as clicks or video views. It's important to recognize that these metrics don't necessarily correlate. Just because a user watched a video doesn't mean they derived satisfaction from it.

Understanding Nonrandom Data Sampling

In practical scenarios, data sampling is often nonrandom and might consist of what is conveniently available, which introduces its inherent biases. Let's take an example from social media advertising to understand this.

Imagine you're an advertiser looking to create a machine learning model that predicts the effectiveness of various ad creatives based on previous campaigns. You might rely on historical data from your company's past social media advertising campaigns. However, this data would predominantly represent the kind of creatives your company has favored in the past and the audiences they have targeted, rather than a representative sample of all possible creatives and all potential audiences.

Let's say your company primarily uses static images for social media ads, and these images are overwhelmingly product-centric. If you train your model on this data, it might perform poorly when predicting the effectiveness of video ads or ads focusing on lifestyle or storytelling. Similarly, if your historical data primarily involves campaigns targeting a particular demographic, your model might struggle to accurately predict the effectiveness of campaigns aimed at a different demographic.

This illustrates how our *convenient sample* can be biased. We end up with a view of ad effectiveness skewed by the preferences and strategies historically employed by our company.

Why do these suboptimal samples occur? There are various reasons.

One reason is underinvestment in data collection. For instance, companies might use readily available historical data without supplementing it with broader data sources. A large part of progress in machine learning has been driven by dedicated efforts to gather high-quality, representative data.

Another reason is that deployment environments often differ significantly from those seen in the data collection phase. This is common in cases where companies expand their offerings to new markets or demographics.

Yet another challenging scenario arises when it is fundamentally difficult to collect unbiased data. This often occurs when our observations are biased due to the actions we take. A situation like this is referred to as *selective labels*. For instance, if you're using data to inform hiring decisions, you typically only have reliable data on individuals you hired, not on those you rejected. Similarly, in lending, you only have repayment data on those to whom you granted loans, not on those you turned down. This type of selective labeling poses a significant challenge for obtaining representative samples, as the very nature of the problem limits the representativeness of the data you can collect.

Addressing Sample Bias

One approach for mitigation that some choose to follow is simply to deploy the model and cross their fingers. This tactic is based on the hope that the sample bias won't critically impact the model's performance in real-world scenarios. It's worth noting, however, that this is often an unreliable and risky method.

A more calculated strategy is to launch the model while also ensuring that a thorough monitoring framework is in place. This framework would allow for continual feedback and additional data collection. As an example, consider a recommendation system on a streaming platform like Netflix. Users can provide direct feedback if the recommended shows or movies don't match their interests. This feedback helps the system understand where it's going wrong and adjust its predictions accordingly.

Another effective strategy is to assign levels of uncertainty to your model's predictions. Instead of having your model produce a binary output, it can have a third option like *uncertain*. For instance, in weather forecasting, if a model cannot definitely predict if there will be rain or sunshine, it could predict *uncertain*. This would then warrant a human meteorologist to examine the data and make the final prediction. Similar systems can be seen in aviation autopilot systems, which hand back control to the human pilot when they encounter uncertain or risky situations.

Finally, the most conservative strategy when dealing with unbalanced samples is to hold back on deploying the model. Instead, resources should be invested in collecting better, more representative data. For instance, in the field of market research, firms might insist on a minimum quality of data before they consider building a predictive model. If the quality isn't up to the mark, the firm might advise their client to enhance their data collection strategies and come back when they have more robust data.

Key Takeaways

- Decoding Models: Understanding the nuts and bolts of machine learning models is important, but it doesn't stop there. It's just as crucial to predict and assess how these models perform when they step out from theory and into practice.

- Two Sides of the Coin: When it comes to binary classification problems, don't fall into the trap of judging a model's performance by its accuracy alone. This narrow viewpoint overlooks the different impacts of errors. Always weigh the importance of false positives and false negatives, acknowledging that each carries its unique consequences.
- The True Cost of Errors: In evaluating the cost of errors, it's easy to focus on the impact on the decision maker. However, remember that individuals and society as a whole also bear the brunt of these errors. So, when you're setting your decision thresholds, think bigger and consider the broader ramifications.
- Redefining Decision Contexts: The setting in which a machine learning model operates can influence the relative costs of different errors. Instead of just fixing thresholds, brainstorm about how you could adjust the decision environment to yield better error tradeoffs and reduce the overall damage of errors.
- Expand Your Horizon: Break free from traditional tradeoffs and consider the wider decision-making environment, which is very much within our control. This could mean altering the decision context to reduce the heftier errors and pave the way for more positive outcomes.

Designing Environments

It's one thing to secure your data, but it's another thing not to be able to connect to anyone else.

Creating a Stage for AI to Shine

In this chapter, we're going to get into the nitty-gritty of how to set things up for machine learning to really do its thing. The big question we're trying to answer is: how can we shape our surroundings so that AI systems can give us their best shot?

To figure this out, let's look back at an idea we talked about earlier. It's an idea that relies on a comparison between two different places; the real world that we live in, and the world of AI. In this idea, the designer's main job is in the real world. They closely watch what's happening, find problems that need fixing, and come up with AI solutions to these problems.

Think of the designer like a football coach. The coach comes up with the game plan, kicks it off, and closely watches how it plays out. On the other side, you've got the machine learning engineers or data scientists. They're like the players on the field, running the plays to make these smart systems work.

In this setup, the designer's role could be compared to a coach's, while the machine learning engineer's job is more like a player's. The coach plans out the big picture, thinking about each detail, taking practical things into account, and picturing the end game. The player, meanwhile, gets in the game and makes the coach's plan a reality, move-by-move, always sticking to the playbook.

But let's make this clear: the coach isn't the one scoring the goals. They're the ones coming up with, planning, and designing the system that the players will put into action. They're in charge of shaping the game environment, creating a space that's perfectly suited to its purpose.

Now, you might be wondering, how do coaches do this in real life? What basic rules guide their game plan? And the big question: can we use these same rules when we're designing environments for machine learning?

To get a better understanding of how to create the best setting for AI, we need to look more closely at how designers, or our coaches, work. How do they start their game plan? What are the main things they think about? If we dig into these questions, we might find some handy tips that can guide us in our goal of designing environments where AI and machine learning can really show us what they've got.

Restricted Outcomes

Unraveling the Restricted Outcomes Quandary

The first terminology we're going to explore is what we call *restricted outcomes*. Our goal is to identify common solutions that have been used to address the restricted outcomes issue. But first, we need to grasp what this truly means.

A restricted outcomes problem pops up when you're trying to predict an outcome Y based on a dataset X. Here's the tricky bit: your predictions influence your decisions, which then impact whether you see the outcome you were initially trying to predict. To make this a bit clearer, let's switch up our real-world example to something different—say, university admissions.

Picture this: You're a university admissions officer. Your job is to decide who gets in and who doesn't. You've got a nifty AI system that helps you predict if a student will drop out or not, based on a bunch of data like high school grades, extracurricular activities, personal essays, and so forth. This prediction is your right-hand man in deciding who gets the thumbs up for admission and who gets a polite "sorry, not this time."

Here's the catch, though. We only get to see if someone actually drops out if they were admitted to the university in the first place, right? We don't have any data on the folks who got turned down because, well, they didn't get admitted to drop out. This is the classic *restricted outcome* issue. Our data is biased because it only includes outcomes for the students who were admitted, not the entire pool of applicants.

So, here's how it goes: You start with an application and feed the details into your AI system. It spits out a prediction, and you use that along with other factors to decide: admission granted or denied. If granted, we'll eventually see if the student dropped out or not. But for those denied admission? Zip. No data. No clue if they might have dropped out or not. This situation is what we call *restricted outcomes*.

The restricted outcomes problem is a real head-scratcher for AI and machine learning, as it affects the quality of the data we have for prediction and decision making. It's a stark reminder of how using AI in the real world often means finding our way through tricky, less-than-ideal situations where the data is influenced by the very decisions it helps to shape.

Deciphering the Puzzle of Restricted Outcomes Problems

Getting a firm handle on when and where this issue crops up is key. This typically happens when we're knee-deep in prediction, not so much in automation. To fully grasp why this is the case, we need to sift through the unique traits of prediction problems that lead to restricted outcomes.

First off, prediction problems rely on observing outcomes. Let's draw up a scenario for automation to give us some context. Say we're dealing with a problem of patient no-shows at doctor's appointments. We might show a patient's details to an expert and ask, "Do you reckon this person will show up for their appointment? What's your take on whether they'll be a no-show or not?" We could gather this kind of information for all patients because we can present all records to a medical professional and ask for their views on potential outcomes.

However, when we switch gears from automation to prediction, things get a bit messy. We're not just asking for opinions or judgments anymore—we're trying to see actual outcomes and predict those outcomes. But our ability to see these outcomes is inherently tied to the processes that enable their observation in the first place. These processes are inevitably shaped by certain decisions, and this stops us from seeing outcomes for the entire population.

So, restricted outcomes typically rear their heads in prediction problems and usually appear when there's a binary decision to be made. One side of that binary decision leads to a complete inability to observe outcomes. For instance, in the patient no-show case, we only see whether people skip their appointments or not if they've made an appointment—not if they never booked one in the first place.

It's useful to ponder other situations that follow this pattern—other problems where outcomes are only visible if one of two decisions is made. Identifying and understanding these scenarios will gear us up to better spot and tackle the restricted outcomes issue in various real-world settings where AI and machine learning systems are put to use.

It's crucial to realize that this issue isn't limited to health care—it's a widespread problem that crops up across various fields and contexts. For example, think about job applications, especially the recruitment process. In this case, you can only see outcomes (job performance) for people who are hired. But this example also adds a little twist to the binary structure we've been discussing so far.

In the realm of job recruitment, if someone doesn't get the job, they might not be able to showcase their performance initially and hence not be hired, but they could impress in another job role later. This means that at some future point—let's say, a year down the line—we might see outcomes that we couldn't capture when we wanted to. This slight delay in observation differs structurally from the patient no-show problem, where, if a patient doesn't book an appointment, we'll simply never know whether they would have shown up or not.

Being able to potentially see outcomes later, while not fully resolving the restricted outcomes issue, does bring a time factor into play that could be used to finetune predictions and, in some cases, lessen the impact of the issue. However, whether this is possible largely hinges on the specific context and the unique structure of the decisions and outcomes at hand.

The main takeaway here is that restricted outcomes problems can take many forms, reflecting the wide range of contexts in which decisions sway the range of outcomes we can see. By understanding these variations, we can design machine learning systems to deal with these scenarios more effectively.

The Importance of the Restricted Outcomes Problem

The real problem with restricted outcomes comes down to not having enough data—or to put it more precisely, missing labels for some parts of the population. This issue is similar to trying to find your way through a maze with half the map missing—you're lacking key information that could radically change your decision making.

Consider those we don't have information on; folks who didn't get a university admission, folks who weren't given a job offer, or people who didn't get the green light for a project proposal. At the heart of the matter is that we don't know what might have unfolded if we'd chosen a different path. In other words, we never get a glimpse of the *what-if* scenarios—the alternative realities—for these folks.

Let's circle back to the university admission example. We never really find out whether those who didn't get admission would have excelled in their studies or not. Even if your model was spot-on in figuring out who would and wouldn't succeed, there's no foolproof way of verifying that. What if the model's off? If you're denying admission to too many people who might've excelled, there's no real way to spot these blunders. You never see the alternate outcomes—what might've happened if you'd chosen differently.

This makes the restricted outcomes issue quite a sneaky problem, as it means missteps might go unnoticed. Without feedback, your models might keep straying off the right path, perpetuating the cycle of flawed decisions. If you're not working with the full dataset, any model you whip up will naturally be a smidge off the mark, which can spell big trouble, especially in critical areas like education or business. So, wrapping our heads around and tackling the restricted outcomes problem is a crucial step in any decision-making process that uses predictive models.

What Are Our Options?

When we start wrestling with the restricted outcomes problem, we need to think hard how we can best navigate this tricky situation. Let's take a few strategies that people often employ in the field. We'll explain each one, discuss how they're utilized in real-world situations, and figure out where each shines the brightest.

The most prevalent method, which seems to me like the least effective solution, is simply to do nothing. This can be called as the *launch and pray* method. The only solid reason to opt for this method is when there's a good chunk of randomness in the way you make decisions.

In other words, this strategy might work decently if your decisions don't consistently leave out a large group of people from your label gathering. To clarify, let's switch gears to the education system and the university admission predictions. In real life, the success of these systems is gauged based on how much admission directors' decisions differ.

Admission directors, being human, naturally have a touch of randomness in their decisions—they all have their unique way of evaluating applicants. If you deployed an admission prediction model for just one director, figuring out how well it's performing would be quite challenging. But, if you had, let's say, 10 directors, all interpreting the predictions in their own way—some might disregard the predictions, others might admit everyone—you'd see a nice variety in decision making. This natural diversity could be used to spot any missteps your model might be making.

Getting into the nuts and bolts of how you'd put this into action is a bit beyond our scope right now, mainly because it's tangled up with complex administrative issues. But the key takeaway here is that an officer doesn't strictly follow your admission prediction. Their decision making isn't as clear-cut as accepting someone if the prediction hits a certain threshold and rejecting them otherwise. Officers' decisions, even though they might be influenced by your predictions, have a random element, deviating from a straightforward high-risk reject system. This variety can be harnessed to check how well your predictions are faring.

So, the launch and pray strategy could work reasonably well if there's enough natural variation and experimentation happening, but it's crucial to highlight the fact that just having that experimentation isn't enough. You must actively engage with the data you're collecting, take a thorough look at it, and figure out how well your model is performing. A significant part of the launch and pray strategy isn't just the launch—it's also the consistent, in-depth evaluation to ensure your model is on target.

Other methods revolve around intentionally collecting a broader array of data. Essentially, this involves collecting data from a more diverse range of individuals before embarking on constructing your actual model. For instance, if you intended to make predictions about online course completion, you might want to look beyond just analyzing the characteristics of those who have completed courses before. You could partner with other online education platforms, acquire their data, or survey a larger group of students, all with the aim of gathering more data to strengthen your model.

Let's consider how this strategy could play out in a wellness context. One initial method could be to randomly offer a wellness program to a wide range of individuals and then monitor anyone who sticks with the program. This data could then be utilized to create your predictive model. While random enrollment might not be the most efficient strategy in the long run, it could provide some valuable data in the short term.

The heart of this approach is the active collection of more diverse data. It's crucial to realize, however, that data collection isn't a one-time task—it's an ongoing process. As the world evolves, your model needs to evolve with it to stay relevant, which means continually updating and gathering data.

This strategy fundamentally involves deliberate experimenting. In fact, some experts have pushed this concept even further by incorporating randomness directly into the decision-making process from the outset. This is similar to A/B testing, where random responses are used to enhance and evaluate models. This method is often used in recommendation systems.

Consider a music streaming platform: it doesn't just play you the top 100 songs it believes you'll enjoy the most. There's a certain level of randomness mixed into your playlist. This intentional variation is designed to test the model's assumptions—whether you skip a song as predicted or, conversely, enjoy something the model didn't think you would. The feedback from these tests helps finetune the model. If a prediction turns out to be incorrect, the error is identified and can be learned from, which wouldn't be possible if the system only played you what it assumed were the top 100 songs you'd enjoy. Therefore, this process of including deliberate randomness offers a more flexible and adaptive way to tackle the restricted outcomes issue.

Interactive AI Systems

Diving Into Interactive Systems

Now, let's discuss a frequently observed setup in machine learning workflows, referred to as interactive AI systems. This setup focuses on the various ways we can incorporate humans into machine learning procedures. The question we often grapple with is: what should human involvement resemble, and what alternatives can we employ?

In a multitude of instances, AI doesn't function independently. Despite common perceptions, many applications involve direct human participation. Only in a handful of areas, such as content moderation and curation on digital platforms, does AI primarily operate to decide what content users view on its own. However, in most other circumstances, humans play an active role. Consequently, we need to contemplate the role humans ought to assume and how to shape the collaboration between human decision makers and the AI intended to assist them.

Much like most aspects of AI deployment, this collaboration exists within a balance; there isn't a one-size-fits-all *best* approach to coordinating human participation. The ideal model will shift based on the context, but this doesn't suggest that a unique interactive AI design is mandated each time a new AI system is developed. In fact, there are several prevalent design models that encapsulate most interactive AI systems.

In the upcoming discussion, we'll delve into what these designs entail, how they function, and when each one might be the most appropriate fit. Grasping these shared components and how to maximize their potential assistance in ensuring that humans and AI can effectively cooperate, amplifying each other's strengths while mitigating possible weaknesses. It's all about achieving a balance that enhances the strengths of both human and AI in decision-making procedures.

Real-World Considerations

The model of guided decision making can be favorably applied to a wide array of situations. For example, consider the health care sector, specifically the role of physicians in diagnosing diseases. Many health care institutions are working on models that can predict the likelihood of a patient developing a certain disease based on their health data. However, such a prediction does not decide the final course of treatment—it is just one of many factors a physician takes into account when making a decision.

This approach is common across a range of sectors. In the financial industry, risk assessment models are used to predict the likelihood of a loan applicant defaulting. In car insurance, AI is increasingly being used to predict potential high-risk drivers. Even in the realm of sports coaching, AI tools predicting an athlete's future performance can provide coaches with additional information to make more informed decisions.

However, when implementing these interactive AI systems, several important factors must be considered. Firstly, the predictions made by the model need to be based on tangible, predictable outcomes. This is essential, to provide valuable and actionable guidance to the human operator.

Take, for instance, the financial sector scenario. A loan officer is given two types of predictive information: a credit score indicating the likelihood of the applicant defaulting on the loan and a financial stability score predicting the applicant's ability to maintain steady income. While these scores provide the loan officer with useful information, they do not dictate a specific course of action.

The main goal of these predictions is to support the human decision maker in making more informed decisions, not to restrict their discretion or replace their judgment. The human operator retains their autonomy and discretion, treating the machine learning model as a tool for decision support rather than a determiner of outcomes. It's this seamless integration of AI intelligence and human judgment that makes interactive AI systems effective in a wide range of situations.

Guidance and Choice in Interactive Systems

When rolling out interactive AI systems, there are several critical factors to keep in mind. As we've discussed, the importance of concrete, predictable outcomes like loan default or financial instability is key. But it's just as crucial to ensure these predictions are as fair as possible.

In these scenarios, you might often run into restricted labels because the model is just helping a human make a decision. The human's decision can greatly influence whether we even see these labels. As a result, many of these situations can look a lot like the restricted outcomes problem.

Another thing to watch out for is overdependence on clear-cut predictions. When you present a numerical forecast, like, say, a 90 percent chance of something happening, it tends to get a lot of weight in the decision-making process. Research shows that these clear-cut forecasts often end up overshadowing other aspects of the decision-making process because they seem so solid. For example, if loan officers are given predicted rates of loan default, they may start placing too much importance to these factors, ignoring other key considerations, like the applicant's work history or personal circumstances.

One way to handle this problem is to see what happens when you give these predictive scores to decision makers. For example, you could run a test where only half of the loan officers see the forecasts and then look at how their decisions compared to those who didn't get the predictive scores. This could give you a good idea of how much influence these scores have on the decision-making process.

On top of all this, the way choices are presented—the *choice architecture*—plays a big role in decision support. Often, setting smart defaults can help guide human operators toward making better decisions. Especially when the system makes the decision-making process more complicated or tricky, people are more likely to stick with the suggested defaults.

For instance, if a system suggests that applicants with scores below five should be approved for a loan as a default, this suggestion is likely to be followed. The results might be different if, instead, the system just gave the score and left the decision completely up to the loan officer. By carefully managing the complexity that the system introduces, you can strategically influence how closely people stick to your default suggestions.

Continuous User Actions

Designing AI Systems for Real-World Challenges

As we're crafting AI systems, we must acknowledge that not all user interactions will be positive and unproblematic. We must anticipate and prepare for users who might seek to exploit the system. An excellent example of this can be seen in the realm of AI customer service bots in online retail.

This dates back to about eight years ago, marking one of the early instances of generative AI used in a highly visible and impactful manner. The intention was to create a bot for an online store that could process customer queries and respond as if it were a real customer service agent. The idea was quite novel and groundbreaking at that time.

The AI bot began by answering innocent queries and providing standard customer service, similar to what one might expect from a human agent. However, because of the bot's design, it could only learn from its interactions with people. Essentially, the bot was a simple language model set loose on the platform, continuously learning from each new interaction. This meant that the bot was constantly evolving.

Nonetheless, this perpetual learning soon became a source of concern. After all, not all customer interactions, particularly in an online retail setting, are positive or polite. Consequently, the bot began mimicking some of these negative behaviors. A significant upset was when the bot started using inappropriate language, a shocking and sadly common behavior seen in online interactions. This occurred because certain customers intentionally manipulated the bot into behaving inappropriately, revealing a major flaw in its design.

Fast forward to 2023, and you might presume we would have learned from those initial missteps when developing new systems. However, an incident involving an AI chatbot in a popular online gaming platform mirrored the same old issues that tripped up the retail bot. Yet again, certain users bombarded the AI chatbot with inappropriate comments, and the AI began parroting this unacceptable behavior, resulting in a significant controversy.

These instances indicate that the challenge of user misbehavior when engaging with public-facing AI has not been eliminated. It's a significant concern that despite the passage of time and numerous high-profile cases, we continue to grapple with solutions. It raises questions as to why these AI models can be so easily manipulated and how quickly they can adopt negative behaviors. It also emphasizes the need to delve deeper into understanding these shortcomings to build more robust and resilient AI systems.

Protecting Your Data in a Manipulative World

The implications we've seen in those examples really underline the need to prudently consider who interacts with our datasets and the potential repercussions if they manipulate them. There's a timeless saying that stands relevant here, "Garbage in, garbage out." If our AI systems are fed tainted or doctored data, their outputs will invariably reflect that.

Consider, for example, the challenges faced by an AI customer service system employed in an e-commerce company. Now, while there are users who offer genuine feedback and valuable input, there might also be a small subset of disgruntled users who deliberately provide misleading information. The tricky part is, the average user doesn't have the time or inclination to correct false data or educate AI bots about the real circumstances. What's more, these attempts to set the record straight probably don't get as much attention as the false or sensational information they're trying to rectify.

The complexity further escalates considering the plethora of topics and products on the e-commerce platform. If a troublemaker zeroes in on a specific product and starts feeding twisted data into the AI system, the AI may end up propagating and amplifying incorrect information.

This problem, known as *data poisoning*, especially applies when malevolent users intentionally infuse misleading data into a model's training set, thereby manipulating the model's behavior. An AI system that learns from user-generated data is particularly vulnerable to such data poisoning.

And it's not just customer service bots at risk. Many AI systems learn from user-generated data, and the repercussions can be far more serious than a bot spreading misinformation. For instance, let's explore some scenarios where AI systems might be at a higher risk from this kind of malicious behavior.

Consider AI in health care, which is a prime example of balancing different data sources. These AI systems learn from both private data gathered under controlled conditions and public data from patients' real-world health records. Each type of data offers unique advantages but also brings along its own set of challenges.

Private data can be better managed, thereby reducing the risk of tampering. However, real-world patient data provides a broader and more accurate picture of various health conditions and their patterns. Still, it's more susceptible to manipulation. The task of striking the right balance between data sources for effective learning is a perpetual challenge.

Another interesting example is a language learning app using AI, which learns from both public and private data. Public data is voluminous and forms the AI's foundational knowledge. But it also brings the risks we've discussed—it could contain misleading or inappropriate language.

To counterbalance this, a smaller amount of controlled private data is used to finetune the AI's behavior, to correct any potential missteps learned from the extensive pool of public data. Despite being smaller in quantity, this supervised data plays a crucial role in ensuring the AI's responses align with societal norms and adhere to the rules.

Blending public and private data sources presents a significant challenge in AI design. The AI must navigate a complex environment, where it needs to learn from an extensive amount of public data but also be meticulously guided by controlled private data to keep its outputs credible. This turns the AI's learning process into a nuanced, ongoing, and delicate task.

The Pitfalls of Public Interaction With AI Systems

As AI systems start to become a bigger part of our everyday lives, the chances for them to be misused also grow. Take ChatGPT as an example. The more people use it to find information or get stuff done, the more valuable it becomes to influence how it behaves. If you put ChatGPT on your own website, you might be able to control what it says.

Think about websites that share information. If the AI model learns from these websites, the content can directly affect how the model behaves. This isn't a new problem—search engines have been dealing with this for years. But it's a new angle on the problem when we're talking about models that generate text. The question of how to make sure these models aren't getting tricked is complex and hard. The more important and widespread these AI systems get, the more tempting it becomes for people to mess with them.

Autocomplete features, like the ones in Google search, are another example. These features, which suggest endings as you type, are hotly contested areas for different groups, including political ones and advertisers. Being able to influence these suggestions can be valuable—for example, imagine being the first suggestion that pops up when a user starts a search.

Autocomplete can also be a way to spread wrong information and lies. For instance, if a person types "Does the COVID vaccine..." into a search bar, different groups might want to guide the following suggestions in different directions. The reasons could be anything from wanting to make money to trying to damage a rival, or even just for fun.

Let's picture a scenario where a competitor wants to spread bad rumors about a MacBook. They could potentially mess with autocomplete to make *MacBook crashes* the top suggestion, changing how people see it—even if just for a little while.

All these examples underline the possible dangers of AI systems learning from public data. They show that we need to keep a close eye on things and take strong steps to block or fight against harmful manipulations. These are important things to think about for any AI design, especially ones that interact directly with the public and have a big impact on society.

Tactics and Instruments

So, how do we tackle this challenge? The solution comes from a bunch of technical tools and methods that are designed to fight off mean tricks on AI systems. A word that often pops up in these chats is *resilience*. Instead of getting lost in the tricky technical details, let's stick to the main point: we're looking to strengthen the toughness and stability of our models.

Imagine this: we want to create an AI model that can tell if someone has pneumonia from chest X-rays. Normally, we would train the model with lots of X-rays showing clear cases of pneumonia. But let's be real, the world outside isn't so simple. A patient's X-ray could have other issues, be unclear, or even misunderstood. So, it's super important to add such variations to our training data, not just clean-cut, perfectly understood pneumonia X-rays. By including blurry or overlapping images, we're basically teaching the model to predict, understand, and deal with any misfeeds that might fool it. The goal here is to make models that are more resilient.

Next, to make our model's predictions even more accurate, we can use a technique that involves multiple models. This concept, known as ensemble learning in the AI world, adds an extra check to our results. For example, if we're trying to create an AI system for disease diagnosis, we can't just rely on X-rays to spot pneumonia. The best system would also use other diagnostic data or even existing patient health records. By using multiple sources of information to confirm a case of pneumonia, we make our system more reliable, which helps keep error at bay.

When it comes to the training data we start with, we have some room for maneuver. However, one rule to stick to when picking inputs is to, whenever possible, go for data that's hard for adversaries to mess with. This principle was central to the original search algorithm of PubMed, which ranked medical research based on how many significant citations it received. The thinking is simple: getting a citation from a top-tier source like The Lancet isn't a walk in the park. If such a well-known source cites a piece of research, it's a solid sign that the research is reliable. So, choosing such hard-to-meddle-with inputs can lead to more trustworthy predictions in a hostile environment.

Apart from these preventive tactics, there's another crucial part of fighting off adversarial or behavior or misleading data, and that's using feedback. Feedback loops are essential for fixing mistakes. For instance, in the case of an AI diagnosis system, a human doctor overriding the AI's diagnosis because it missed a symptom is extremely valuable feedback. It's a sign that a mistake has been made, and we need to do something to fix it. This kind of feedback is always helpful, but it's worth its weight in gold when we're dealing with adversarial actions.

Lastly, it's key to stay on top of the big picture. Regular manual checks of a subset of instances classified by the model—be it a pneumonia diagnosis, a flagged anomaly, or any other label—can help us see if the model's decisions match up with human ones. We need to be alert to new adversarial tricks that humans can spot but that the model might miss. Plus, it's important to keep an eye on key performance indicators—for example, the total number of correct diagnoses. A drop in this number could either mean there are fewer cases or that our diagnosis efficiency has taken a hit. Figuring out which one it is can be key to keeping our system on point and effective.

Cyclical Refinement

A Path to Innovation

Diving into new areas with machine learning, especially when we're dealing with new industries or applications, can often feel like we're explorers mapping out new territory. Imagine this in the world of modern farming technology. Machine learning models are increasingly being used to improve farming methods, with devices analyzing a wide range of data, like soil quality, weather patterns, and crop growth, among other things.

But the problem is, before these smart farming tools came along, we didn't have a ton of detailed data on how different soil types or weather conditions could impact a crop's growth. So, if we're starting with hardly any historical data, how do we go about building machine learning models that are reliable?

This is where *cyclical refinement* comes into play. This concept recognizes the fact that developing a machine learning model is not a straight-line process from Point A to B. Instead, it's a kind of cycle—one where we build a basic model, put it to work, collect data, learn from this data, and then tweak the model. This loop could go on and on, with every cycle making the model better and better.

In the world of smart farming, developers probably started with very basic models. These initial models would be trained on whatever data they had at hand—maybe data from controlled experiments in labs or small-scale farm setups. Once these early models were up and running, they'd start collecting real-world data from farms, adding tons of new data points to their existing datasets.

With all this fresh data, which is way more varied and detailed than what the developers started with, they'd then go back and refine the models. As the models go through each cycle of refinement, they get better at recognizing patterns and making predictions based on a broader and more representative dataset.

The key thing to remember from the cyclical refinement pattern is that it's totally okay to start with a basic model and limited data. What's more important is setting up a way for your model to learn and improve over time. The beauty of cyclical refinement is in its evolution—it's all about continuous learning and adjusting, just like the way we humans learn. By using this approach, developers can keep improving their models, making them more effective and reliable over time, even if they started with hardly any data.

Idea to Iterative Enhancement

Creating a system for spotting fake reviews wasn't exactly a walk in the park. It's a classic example of the *chicken or the egg* dilemma we often see in machine learning. You need a working system to draw in users, but you also need users to create the data you need for the system to work. So how did pioneers in the field, like Yelp, get around this problem?

Their trick was to first create a platform that offered features not necessarily related to machine learning to attract users. When Yelp first launched, it didn't have a system to detect fake reviews. However, it provided a host of other useful features, like allowing users to find and rate local businesses. These features drew in users, creating a base for data collection. Even though users weren't signing up to Yelp to help catch fake reviews, their interactions on the platform provided valuable data that could be used for this purpose.

With a collection of historical data from users' interactions with Yelp, an initial model was built. This could be called a *first attempt* model. This model could estimate how many potential fake reviews would pop up per business per day. But this early data wasn't labeled. It wasn't clear which reviews were fake and which were genuine, just routine activities. Still, it was a beginning.

This first-stage model offered a way to test the sensitivity of the fake review detection algorithm. By understanding how often it would flag reviews, developers could tweak their model by adjusting certain limits. If it was flagging too many reviews each day, it meant the system needed stricter criteria.

With a basic model and an understanding of how sensitive it was, the next step was to put it to the test. Usually, features like this are first introduced to a small group of users. This could be staff, tech-savvy testers, or even some daring early users. A critical part of this phase was including a way for users to give feedback. This allowed developers to gather important data on how well the model was working: how often were genuine reviews flagged? How often did it miss fake reviews?

Adjusting the frequency of flagged reviews was a key part of the feedback loop. If you set the bar too high, you end up annoying your testers with too many false positives. Set it too low, and you might miss important instances of actual fake reviews. Striking the right balance was critical to prevent users from ditching the platform due to too many false alerts or a lack of trust in its capabilities.

With a feedback system in place, developers could adjust and refine the model in cycles. Each cycle was an opportunity to improve the model's performance, using the feedback and new data provided by users. This process of cyclical refinement wasn't limited to spotting fake reviews; similar strategies have been used for other applications on the platform, like detecting inappropriate content.

The application of cyclical refinement in the world of online reviews highlights its potential when dealing with situations where you're starting with little or no historical data. It shows how innovative platforms can effectively develop and refine machine learning models, even when starting from scratch. The development of fake review detection on Yelp is a shining example of the power of cyclical refinement and the ongoing process of learning, improving, and enhancing.

Wrap Up—Chapter Recap

In the earlier chapters, we took a detailed look at shaping the most optimal environment for machine learning applications. We've explored four major design blueprints—restricted outcomes, interactive AI systems, continuous user actions, and cyclical refinement. Each of these introduces its own vibe, opportunities, and challenges. Having a solid understanding of these offers us the toolkit to maximize machine learning and tackle its challenges head-on. Let's pause for a moment to revisit these blueprints and truly comprehend their value.

Restricted outcomes is all about those situations where you get to see only bits and pieces of the result, not the whole picture. It's similar to trying to understand a movie plot by watching just a trailer—you get a glimpse, but much of it is still hidden. The challenge here is deciphering what's behind the unseen parts. How do we interpret the bigger scenario from a limited dataset? How do we ensure that the insights we draw from our small view are genuinely reflective of the full picture?

Interactive AI systems are about integrating human judgment into the equation. These systems marry human intuition with machine accuracy to bring about superior results. However, this approach isn't without its own set of challenges. How do we best incorporate human expertise into a machine learning system? What's the perfect balance between automation and human intervention, and how do we strike a balance between the need to scale and maintaining the quality of human input?

When we talk about continuous user actions, we're dealing with deliberate disruptions, or inputs that will lead to wrong outcomes. This is where someone or something is purposely meddling with the training data or model inputs. It's like a game of chess, where our machine learning applications must constantly stay ahead of those attempting to checkmate them. The main questions here are: how do we create models that can withstand these disruptions, and how do we prepare for these challenges without getting stuck in a never-ending cycle of modifications?

Finally, we come to cyclical refinement. This is where systems mature and evolve over time, learning from past experiences. This often happens when we start with a small amount of data, and the system has to learn and progress as it collects more data. But, this methodology also brings some significant considerations. How do we establish a beneficial feedback loop to guide the system's learning? How do we strike a balance between making too many changes, which could destabilize the system, and the need for continuous improvement?

It's vital to keep in mind that these blueprints don't encompass everything. There are countless other methods to design machine learning systems that we haven't delved into. However, the four blueprints we've discussed often crop up in numerous machine learning applications.

Understanding these blueprints does more than just equip you with useful knowledge; it transforms the way you perceive what's possible. It prompts you to rethink what machine learning applications can and can't accomplish in various scenarios. Being aware of these blueprints can serve as a reality check as well as a source of innovative ideas.

Moreover, comprehending these blueprints can enhance your ability to design systems that can tackle the issues we've examined. This will help you in making informed decisions and building robust, reliable systems. It can also shed light on why others may have made certain design choices. Understanding these blueprints offers you a lens to scrutinize and learn from others' decision making, enhancing your prowess in understanding machine learning systems.

As we conclude this deep dive into machine learning design blueprints, it's beneficial to reflect on what they offer and the challenges they present. These blueprints serve as our guide, steering us through the vast, sophisticated world of machine learning.

Responsible AI and Privacy

It may be complex, but it's not complicated.

Responsible AI

Tackling Discrimination, Privacy, and Morality in AI

As we start dipping our toes into responsible AI, we find ourselves standing at a pretty interesting fork in the road. Two big ideas—discrimination and privacy—are staring right at us. Now, they might look like different problems, but when it comes to AI and all this data we're collecting, they're just two different sides of the same coin. And as we start digging into these, we'll also start seeing the bigger picture around AI policy.

Think of responsible AI like being a tightrope walker. It's all about balance and trying to guess what's going to happen next. Will the results be good or bad? It's a tough call, and honestly, it's kind of a matter of opinion. Like that tightrope walker, we're all just trying to stay upright, and it's okay if we wobble a bit. My job here is to help guide you through this complex landscape or to act like a safety net. But remember, we might not always agree on what's good or bad. And that's okay. These differences in opinions are what make our journey interesting.

First up on our journey is the tricky subject of discrimination. Let's look at how, despite our best intentions, machine learning can sometimes end up causing a bit of a stir around discrimination. And, of course, we'll try to find ways to dodge that.

The word discrimination brings up a lot of feelings about past and current injustices. From New York to New Delhi, people all over the world deal with discrimination based on things like race, gender, sexuality, ethnicity, religion, and even caste. Despite laws trying to wipe out discrimination, it's a sad fact that it's still around, causing real differences in people's lives.

Discrimination has changed over time. It's moved from the obvious bias of the past, like those old ads that targeted specific groups, to a more subtle form that's a lot harder to spot. It gets really tricky when this sort of discrimination is hiding in the big decisions made by companies.

Consider this: studies have found that when employers get two identical resumes with different names, they're more likely to call back the ones with *white-sounding* or male names. This is a hidden form of modern discrimination, and it's really hard to figure out where it's coming from. This makes fighting discrimination really challenging.

Now, people often think that computers, as they don't have human biases, are neutral and won't discriminate. But hold up a second. Are we really sure about that? What if these machine learning systems, when trained on data that's already got biases, just end up repeating the same mistakes? Think about it this way: machine learning is like a mirror. It shows us the past. If we don't like what we see in that reflection, it's not the mirror's fault. It's due to the practices of the past.

A Deeper Dive Into Challenges and Lessons

The well-known MIT researchers Joy Buolamwini and Timnit Gebru decided to take a close look at the accuracy of several facial recognition systems available in the market. They weren't messing around either, deciding to test models from big players like Microsoft and IBM. Using a dataset of images of politicians from all over the world, they put these models to the test to see how well they did.

What they found was really surprising. You see, these companies often boast about an amazing 99 percent accuracy rate. But Buolamwini and Gebru found out that this near-perfect rate didn't apply to everyone. The systems struggled more when trying to identify women with darker skin tones compared to men with lighter skin tones.

So, why did these top-notch systems stumble when it came to certain groups of people? Was it intentional bias? No, it wasn't anything like that. The truth is, the systems were mostly trained on images of men with lighter skin tones. So, they naturally did better for this group.

This study throws light on a big problem in machine learning—the data we use to train the models isn't always representative. If the data is biased toward certain groups, the models will do a great job for those groups and not so well for others. The fix seems simple enough: make the training data more diverse. Add more data from those groups that the model has a tough time with, and it'll get better. Big tech companies like Microsoft and IBM have realized this problem and are actively trying to fix it.

Tackling this issue is really important, especially when you think about how these systems are used in real life. Let's say a police department is using facial recognition tech to identify suspects. What if the tech messes up? Well, there have already been cases of people being wrongly arrested because of these errors. That's why some places, like the San Francisco police, have decided to limit the use of facial recognition tech by the police in certain cases.

But, it's not just about making facial recognition work perfectly for everyone. We also need to think about whether it's okay to use this tech in certain situations at all. Given the chance of mistakes, should we really be relying entirely on this tech for things like arrests? We should have a more thorough checking process, backed up with more evidence.

This situation serves as a tough reminder of how important it is to check how well machine learning models work for all important social groups, especially when these models are used by the public. We need to understand how a model works for different ages, races, genders, and so on. This way, we can make sure it's fair and cut down on bias. This hard lesson is now seen as a must-do in the world of machine learning.

A Maze of Challenges and Uncomfortable Tradeoffs

The Internal Revenue Service (IRS) offers a powerful example of bias within AI. It was found that their system had a negative impact on Black Americans, predominantly those who used the Earned Income Tax Credit. This throws up a crucial question: How can we assess the effects of machine learning models on different racial groups, especially when explicit racial data isn't easily available?

Lots of companies are nervous about collecting and storing data related to their users' race. There are concerns around misuse and trust issues. But at the same time, these companies need to ensure fairness across all racial groups. To navigate this tightrope, some have adopted predictive approaches based on other available data. For instance, LinkedIn estimates a user's gender from their first name to balance gender in search results. In a similar vein, some groups employ Bayesian Improved Surname and Geocoding (BISG), a method that predicts race and ethnicity using users' surnames and geographic locations.

Another possible solution is to ask a subset of users to voluntarily provide their demographic data for auditing purposes. However, this requires a high level of trust. Companies like Airbnb and LinkedIn have started to explore this route.

But tackling AI bias isn't as simple as just dividing performance metrics by social groups, identifying disparities, and fixing them. The case of the COMPAS algorithm, used widely in the United States to predict reoffending likelihood and pretrial no-shows, highlights this complexity.

ProPublica, a news outlet, decided to evaluate COMPAS, focusing on error rates among different racial groups. They found that the false-positive rate was roughly twice as high for African American defendants compared to white defendants. The false-negative rate was about half as much.

At first, this may seem like an obvious case of bias. But, if you dig a bit deeper, it's more complex. For one, the rearrest rate for African American defendants was higher than that for white defendants. This higher false-positive rate for African Americans might just be reflecting this higher rearrest rate.

The case throws up a tough dilemma when dealing with different base rates across populations. Decision makers have a tricky choice. They can either accept varying error rates for different groups or set different thresholds for what counts as high risk for different racial groups. Neither choice is without issues, highlighting the complex and sensitive nature of dealing with bias in AI systems.

A Dance Between Social Inequities, Predictive Models, and Policy Choices

Simply broadening our data collection doesn't necessarily wipe out biases in machine learning models. If the data we're drawing from—like arrest records—are skewed, machine learning models just mirror and reproduce these biases, no matter how well balanced the data appears. In essence, machine learning isn't a magic pill for social inequalities; it only mirrors the biases present in its training data. Therefore, there's no standard, one-size-fits-all solution to fix bias in machine learning. After all, these models, as sophisticated as they are, can't remedy social issues with mathematical adjustments alone.

In addition to checking for model bias, it's equally crucial to see how these models operate within the context in which they're deployed. Models should be analyzed as components of larger systems, not standalone entities. For instance, if models are used to allocate rides to minimize court no-shows, we need to understand how providing a ride influences someone's likelihood of turning up in court. However, using these predictions also forces policy decisions into the mix, like how to prioritize ride allocation based on predicted impacts.

In these scenarios, it's the policy, not the model, that may inadvertently introduce bias. Take Santa Clara County, California, as an example. The relationship between race and residential location—and consequently, the cost of rides—led to racial disparities in ride allocation. The policy was set up to boost court appearances within a budget by ranking defendants based on the predicted impact per dollar spent. However, the overlap of racial distribution and ride costs unintentionally resulted in some racial groups benefiting more than others from the program. Even though the predictions of court appearance likelihood and the effect of offering a ride were accurate, the policy didn't address the question of how to distribute a fixed budget in a fair, nondiscriminatory manner.

There are various ways to handle such a situation. One could opt for a completely random ride allocation strategy, which effectively ignores the goal of maximizing court appearances. This approach ensures equal chances of receiving government aid, regardless of race. Santa Clara County initially employed this randomization strategy until they got a clearer picture of who needed rides the most. With this knowledge in hand, they faced the complex task of balancing factors like residential locations or ride costs within their fixed budget constraints. Ultimately, the difficult policy decisions about resource allocation unveiled the interplay of social inequities, predictive models, and policy execution, highlighting the sophisticated ballet between these components.

Tradeoffs, Goals, and Ethics

Working with AI systems often means juggling some tradeoffs. In an ideal world, we'd be able to handle these tradeoffs, lining them up with our goals and ethical rules. In this chapter, we'll dive into a strategy to find a balance between making the system work better and ensuring fairness for everyone.

Imagine these tradeoffs as points on a graph. One axis shows the extra number of people who benefit from an AI tool (like seeing more people show up to court). The other axis shows how equitably the benefits are spread across different groups of people. Once you've got your AI model working, you can draw this graph to see the balance between these two important factors. Each point on the graph represents a specific policy choice—a delicate balance between making things work well and making things fair.

This graph really brings out the need to make tough choices between things like efficiency, accuracy, influence, and fairness among different groups. AI lets us shine a light on these tradeoffs and tweak them. By using predictive models, we can build a system that clearly shows our preferred balance on the graph, matching up with policy goals.

Remember, this isn't just about ethics. It also has a big impact on how we make rules. People might not agree on where the best balance is on the graph. But, they should agree that the graph should exist, balancing key factors that can be measured. Understanding this leads to smarter policy choices.

AI pushes us to put a number on tradeoffs, giving us a better picture of what our decisions lead to. For example, if a judge has to decide who gets certain benefits, the hidden tradeoffs in their choices might be unclear. But with the precise predictions offered by AI, we can put a number on these tradeoffs. As this approach spreads to policy making, we can handle these tradeoffs more fairly, avoiding having to rely on someone's unclear decision-making process.

A real-world example of these tradeoffs is the way ads are auctioned online. It's really important to understand the predictive models being used and be aware of any potential unfair outcomes these models might lead to.

Online ad auctions work in a pretty simple way. When you visit an online platform, advertisers bid to show you their ads. The platform uses machine learning to guess how likely you are to click on each ad. It then shows you the ad that's expected to bring in the most money—the product of the bid amount and the click chance.

But where could unfairness sneak in? A well-known case at Facebook gives us a useful example. Different ads, ranging from shoes to job postings, targeted different groups of people. This led to a situation where women mainly saw ads for shoes, while men saw more job ads, accidentally creating an imbalance.

In 2018, the U.S. Department of Housing and Urban Development took Facebook to court over these differences in ad distribution. Ads for housing, jobs, and credit are regulated by federal law, and a settlement required Facebook to make sure these types of ads were equally shown to all groups of people. This policy meant making a tradeoff—giving up some of Facebook's revenue to ensure equal ad exposure across all groups.

Understanding the Dollars and Cents Behind AI Algorithms

To start wrapping our heads around the tangled web of AI algorithms and the economic theories they involve, let's imagine a situation with an AI ad algorithm. Let's call our user Sigal. Sigal could be shown a shoe ad that brings in U.S.\$3. Or, she might see a job ad that makes a bit less—U.S.\$2. At its core, the algorithm is built to get the most out of the bid value, and straying from this goal could mean losing money.

But this calculation involves more than just the bid value. It also takes into account an estimate of how likely a user is to interact, usually measured by the click-through rate. An ad with less user interaction naturally makes less money. So, when companies tweak these algorithms to fight biases, they also need to think about the possible economic consequences.

Regulators also play a key role in keeping balance in AI systems. While they might not know as much about AI as tech companies, their insights and decisions are really important. They don't make decisions on their own; they're backed up by technical consultations with a bunch of experts. Remember that these regulators often work within practical limits and duties, like avoiding collecting demographic data.

So, any criticism of a regulator's actions should be seen in light of the limits and the principles we've talked about in this chapter. While regulators are making headway in tackling the ethical issues of AI, the task is tough given the complex and multilayered nature of the technology.

The impact of AI systems can be far-reaching. Predictions and actions for one person can start a chain reaction and potentially create imbalances for others. So, if you come across an AI product that claims to be *unbiased* or *fair*, approach it with a healthy dose of doubt. Ask for clarity around these buzzwords and question what concrete steps have been taken to reduce bias.

For instance, an AI system might promise equal selection rates across different groups of people, but this brings up questions about potential impacts and legal issues. As AI gets more complex, companies have to take responsibility for any unfair practices that their AI models might lead to.

Right now, U.S discrimination law is reactive, meaning someone has to make a complaint before anything happens. While there haven't been many successful cases where algorithmic discrimination was proven, it's likely that a lot of models are close to breaking the law.

To wrap up this part of the chapter, there are a few important points to keep in mind. First, AI models, based on historical data, can unintentionally reflect historical biases. They're not a magic solution for societal issues; they just mirror existing imbalances. Second, the context in which a model is used is crucial and can greatly affect outcomes. Even models without bias can create imbalances if they're launched into a biased system.

Whenever possible, these tradeoffs should be made clear, fostering a culture of transparency and accountability. Lastly, always approach claims of *unbiased* or *fair* AI systems with a healthy dose of skepticism. Question the definitions, challenge the steps taken to fight bias, and never just take these claims at face value.

Privacy in the Realm of AI

Unraveling Privacy With an AI Impact

When we say *privacy*, people think of all sorts of things. Some might think it means keeping their chats with friends secret. Others might think it means having the right to be left alone. Some might see it as controlling who gets to see their personal information. So, privacy isn't just one thing; it's a bunch of related ideas. As we talk about AI and machine learning, we'll try to shed some light on these different parts of privacy and why the distinctions are so important.

Why does privacy become a big deal when we talk about AI? The main issue is that AI needs data—lots of it. This data can tell a lot about our lives. Every time we use data to build AI or machine learning models, we might be giving away some of our secrets. This brings up a question: do we see this as a necessary tradeoff for the progress of AI? Is it hard to keep privacy intact while building high-performance AI systems?

A good example is the Cambridge Analytica scandal. This company took user data from Facebook and used it to target political ads in 2016. They wanted to sway public opinion and election results. They tried to build accurate machine learning systems, but they stomped all over people's privacy. Even though they clearly broke Facebook's rules, the damage was done.

Events like this have pushed the industry to be more careful about privacy. This change is due to new laws like the General Data Protection Regulation (GDPR) and big fines. Look at Facebook; they've been hit with big fines for their earlier relaxed attitude to privacy. Their privacy policy changed a lot, from being almost nonexistent in 2013 to very careful by 2018.

As we explore privacy and machine learning, we need to rethink our old beliefs. We need to think more about how these privacy issues shape our view of AI and how big tech companies are changing their strategies.

Understanding the puzzle of privacy means looking at its different interpretations and the contexts they work in. It's not just about keeping our personal chats private or staying anonymous. Privacy, especially in AI, is about finding the balance between chasing tech advancements and our basic right to control our personal information. It's a big mix of ethical, societal, and tech factors that we need to think about and handle carefully. This isn't just for academics; it's a crucial part of understanding the role and responsibilities of AI in our world.

50 Shades of Gray in Privacy

A lot of folks think that information is either private or public, and that's it. But it's not that simple. In reality, there's a whole range of how accessible information can be. For example, encrypted data is technically public, but it's not as easy to get to as the stuff on your public social media page. Looking at information this way helps us understand privacy better.

Let's look at a real-life example. A group of researchers once collected data from OkCupid, an online dating site, for a study. Even though these profiles were public and anyone with the Internet could see them, people got pretty mad when this data was collected and shared publicly. This shows that even when information is technically public, we might still want some privacy around it.

How we understand what's private or public is a tricky balancing act. And as technology gets more advanced, this balance can shift. Imagine if the cops used heat-sensing tech to look inside your home from their car parked outside—would that invade your privacy? As tech gets better, we need to update our definitions and standards of privacy.

An interesting way to keep privacy online is the *no index* request. This is a tool that lets websites tell search engines not to list certain pages, making them harder to find. While this can protect sensitive information, it can also be misused. For instance, TurboTax used a *no index* request to hide its free version from Google search results, making it tricky for users to find.

When we think about how to protect privacy in datasets, the first solution we often think of is *anonymization*. The idea is simple—just remove things like names and addresses from the dataset, and then it's safe for public use. But, as we've learned from past events, this basic approach to privacy, which became popular in the mid-1990s, doesn't always work.

Anonymization doesn't consider all the complexities of privacy. It assumes that by taking out personally identifiable information, we've completely protected privacy. But in today's world of big data, people can often be reidentified by cross-referencing *anonymized* datasets with other public information. Privacy isn't just a one-and-done thing but an ongoing process. As we use more and more data, we need to make our privacy strategies more sophisticated and flexible.

The Web of Privacy

When AOL once shared what it thought was anonymous search data, things didn't go as planned. They gave unique numbers to users, tying them to their searches. But *The New York Times*, working with this *anonymous* data, was able to find a specific woman by analyzing her search history and figuring out where she was. This incident powerfully showed us that just using anonymization doesn't really keep our privacy safe.

Netflix, a giant tech company, had a similar problem. They shared movie-watching data they thought was anonymous for research purposes. However, researchers showed it could be cross-referenced with IMDb data to figure out who the users were.

These cases highlight the fact that just anonymizing data isn't enough to deal with privacy concerns. To really protect privacy, it's not enough to just remove personal identifiers. We need to look at the type of data we're dealing with and use other strategies, like adding noise to make the data less easy to trace back to a person.

When we mix privacy and machine learning, we face a whole new set of challenges. For example, can we get personal details or specifics about the training data from the machine learning model itself? This was a big question when the Getty Images and AI model outputs case came to light. The models were churning out results very similar to the training images, suggesting that the model had somehow *memorized* the training data.

Worse still, this could potentially lead to leaking sensitive data. Think about autocomplete features on our devices, driven by machine learning models that learn from our typing habits. They could accidentally learn and suggest sensitive details like credit card numbers or passwords.

To tackle this, we add noise to the text data and program in specific rules to avoid storing and suggesting sensitive details. This step helps ensure privacy but also highlights potential pitfalls. Even machine learning models with good intentions can reveal sensitive details about the people whose data was used in their training.

In fields like health care, where privacy is essential, such weak spots could cause serious problems. Recent studies show it's possible to pull out patients' genetic markers from models predicting the right medication dosage, which is a scary privacy risk.

So what's the big lesson here? Simply, models can give away information. They reveal details about the people in the dataset. While this is partly what they're designed to do—they're supposed to learn from data—it becomes a huge privacy issue if it gives away identifiable details about people. As we navigate the world of AI and machine learning, we need to remember that privacy isn't just something to consider; it's a necessity. Achieving it isn't simple, and anonymization is just a basic first step. Privacy is a complex issue that needs a complex response.

To wrap things up, the relationship between privacy and AI shows us the challenges we face in making tech that's good for society without stepping on people's rights. It's a constant balancing act that needs our ongoing attention. As AI continues to become a bigger part of our lives, it's super important for both organizations and individuals to prioritize privacy. We should aim to build AI systems that are responsible and that respect and protect our data.

Key Takeaways

- Unexpected Results: AI models have a big influence on society, and sometimes, this can lead to unexpected outcomes. For instance, algorithms might accidentally strengthen existing biases. This shows that developers need to think about potential issues when they're making these models.
- How AI Affects the Economy: AI algorithms can have serious effects on the economy. When we're trying to tweak these algorithms to lessen bias, we need to think about possible economic side effects.
- Why Regulation Matters: Regulators play a key role in keeping AI systems balanced. They bring a certain level of knowledge to AI, and their decisions are made smarter by technical input from different experts.
- What Privacy Really Means: Privacy is a complex idea that people can interpret in different ways. It can mean staying anonymous or having control over personal information. As AI tech relies a lot on data, it's extremely important to think about privacy.
- The Spectrum of Information Access: Information privacy exists on a spectrum, with encrypted data on the one end and public data on the other. As tech keeps evolving, our views on privacy need to change too.

- Why Anonymization Isn't Enough for Privacy: Just anonymizing data doesn't fully protect privacy. Just because we remove personally identifiable information, it doesn't mean a dataset is safe to share with the public.
- The Danger of Models Leaking Information: Machine learning models can accidentally reveal sensitive details about the people whose data they were trained on. This means we need better techniques to protect privacy.
- The Need for Transparency and Accountability: When we're developing AI systems, we need to focus on transparency and accountability. If an AI system claims to be *unbiased* or *fair*, we should question it. We should ask for real steps taken to reduce bias.
- The Changing Concept of Privacy: As AI and machine learning keep advancing, our understanding of privacy needs to keep up. Privacy is more than just a concern—it's a must-have. Protecting it requires complex solutions to a complex problem.

Now What?

Well, the best way to predict the future is to create it. It's as simple and profound as that. If you're wondering about what AI will look like in the next five years, how our lives will be mixed with tech in the next 10 years, or if our kids will still need to learn to read and write without digital help, you need to really think about your plans for tomorrow. Consider what jobs you'll do when you get to work, the top things you'll focus on in your day, and the choices you'll make in meetings. What we do today will shape what happens tomorrow.

Let's be clear about one thing with AI; it's not human, and it never will be. Take humor, for example. They say, if you want someone to think you're funny, don't tell them you're funny; tell them a joke. AI, as it is right now, doesn't tell jokes—it tells us it can create jokes. But can it really be funny? It's like trying to tickle yourself. You know where you're most ticklish, you might be really good at tickling your kids until they can't stop laughing, but no matter how good you are, you can't make yourself laugh by tickling yourself.

And why's that? It's because laughing, like lots of other human experiences, isn't just about the physical part. It's about the unexpected, the surprise, and the emotional connection with the person making you laugh. These are things that AI, even with all its algorithms and computing power, can't copy.

AI is an incredibly useful tool, but it's crucial to remember that it's just that—a tool. It can make our lives easier, automate boring tasks, and even copy human behavior to some extent. But it doesn't have the human touch, the spontaneity, the ability to really understand and feel the human experience. It's a feature, not a bug. This isn't a failure of AI— it's just a way to remember the unique, priceless qualities that make us human.

Let me tell you a story from my teen years. It's one of those tales that would pop up in school hallways, with no one really knowing where it came from; maybe it was just an urban myth, but it was a really cool story anyway. The story was about an English homework given to a group of middle school kids, who were asked to write an essay on a simple topic: *What is bravery?*

As I started writing this book, I found myself thinking about what would happen if a student today, with the power of AI in their hands, asked a language model to give them a hand with this homework. I decided to test it, asking a GPT chatbot to describe *bravery*. Here's what it spit out:

> Bravery is a basic human virtue defined by the ability to face fear, danger, uncertainty, or hardship with guts, willpower, and toughness. It is the quality that lets people take on challenges, take risks, and chase their dreams despite possible obstacles or bad outcomes. Bravery is not the lack of fear, but winning against it. It involves recognizing fear but deciding not to let it control what you do.

While this answer isn't wrong or useless, there's something kind of bland about this response, right? It's missing the creative spark, the personal touch, the human view that can turn a regular essay into a standout one.

The kid, asked to write an essay on bravery, handed in a paper with just three words: "This is bravery." Yep, you heard right. That was the whole essay. "This is bravery." The mark this bold kid got changes depending on who you ask back in my hometown—some say full marks, others say none. But the mark isn't the main point of the story. The real deal is about the spark of creativity, the human ability to think differently, and to do something no one saw coming. This kind of innovation is something that AI, as it is now or even as we will see it in the near future, can't copy.

AI can do a ton of stuff, but it's not ready to come up with truly fresh, creative ideas. It's a tool, not a substitute for human creativity and gut feelings. This is a crucial difference to bear in mind as we keep bringing AI into different parts of our lives and work.

I've been chewing over the complex dance between talent, recognition, and fame since I heard an awesome analysis of fame while driving to Eilat for a vacation with my family. The drive was a long six hours on a pretty dull desert road, and we were listening to a fascinating podcast called *The Obvious Thing*. The episode was called "Why is the Mona Lisa so famous?" It might seem like a weird question on the surface. After all, it's a piece of art by the legendary Leonardo da Vinci. But think about it—lots of artists have made masterpieces, so why has the Mona Lisa become so famous?

I'd say that the Mona Lisa's fame has more in common with Kim Kardashian's fame than with the fame of, let's say, Lionel Messi or Elton John. Interesting, right? Let me explain. Messi is known worldwide because he's one of the best football players who ever stepped on the field. Elton John, in the same way, is a legendary figure in music, whose songs have touched people across generations. The link between their amazing talents and their fame is pretty easy to see—they're insanely good at what they do, and their fame is a direct result of their brilliance.

AI, as we know it today, could probably get this clear connection. It could crunch the numbers, understand the cause-and-effect relationship between being great and being famous, and maybe even predict who'll be famous in the future based on visible talent and skill. It's pretty likely that AI could even spot a rising star in a field that's not football or music and forecast their rise to fame.

But here's where things get complicated. Why is Kim Kardashian famous? What specific talent or skill shot her into the spotlight? She got a bit famous, showed up on TV, got a bit more famous, showed up on more TV, and the cycle kept going until she hit crazy levels of fame. But is her fame because she's insanely good at something, as our logical model would suggest? The answer isn't a simple *yes* or *no*, and I'm not totally sure AI could understand the subtleties of her fame.

Yet, whether AI gets it or not, Kim Kardashian's fame is a hard fact. It's a sign of the unpredictable, multifaceted, and often confusing nature of human society, and a reminder that AI, for all its power and promise, still has a long journey ahead in really understanding the complexities of human behavior and social happenings.

So, how do we explain the mystery of the Mona Lisa? Other paintings are bigger, some might say more beautiful, older, and made by more accomplished painters. We even have AI-made art that could arguably be seen as more pleasing to the eye than Da Vinci's masterpiece. But somehow, the Mona Lisa is on top of this artistic mountain, a symbol of excellence and value that's so high, it's basically priceless.

We can make guesses about why it's in this special position. Maybe it's because of the dramatic story of it being stolen and then found again, an event that threw it into the spotlight. Maybe it's the effect of time and being seen again and again, giving it a halo effect that's made it more and more famous to the point of near worship. But the truth is, there's no simple answer or final explanation for the Mona Lisa's unmatched fame. And if we, as people, have a hard time explaining it, it's unlikely that AI, with what it can do right now, could solve this mystery.

In a kind of funny nod to the Mona Lisa's status, think about this: Kim Kardashian, even with her huge worldwide fame, went to the Louvre Museum to snap a selfie with the Mona Lisa. The Mona Lisa, of course, didn't need to return the favor. The pecking order is obvious—even famous people want to soak up some of the reflected glory of the world's most famous painting.

While this story adds a touch of humor to our conversation, it also highlights an important point: AI has its limits when it comes to getting the finer points of human behavior, social phenomena, and the sometimes illogical things we value and look up to. It's an admission of the subtleties, irrationalities, and emotional complexities that are the foundation of our culture—things that, for now, are mostly out of AI's reach.

So, what's next? It's easy: get to work on building an incredible world—not just for us, but for the generations that will come after us. Go for it with every tool you have: whether that's AI, machine learning, deep learning, or any other high-tech that's going to come along. Use these tools to make yourself more efficient and improve your effectiveness in everything you do.

But don't forget about three important questions you should always be asking:

How does AI work?
What is AI really good at?
What are the things we shouldn't leave up to AI?

How does it work? What is it really good at? And what can't it do? Understand that AI, as smart as it is, isn't quite ready to crack a good joke just yet. And remember that your own ability to come up with new ideas is better than any AI that's around right now—and probably will be for a pretty long time.

Accept that while AI can play a big part in helping you with your strategic planning—especially if you're looking to take advantage of more capabilities or markets—you might want to think twice before relying on it completely for groundbreaking, game-changing ideas. AI can help guide you, offering insights based on data that might help you make decisions. But when it comes to real innovation—those game-changing, shake-up-the-industry ideas—there's still a big gap between AI and the human brain.

Make the most of what AI can do, but don't forget about what it can't do. Aim for a balance between machine intelligence and human creativity in your pursuit of success. This is how we will build a future that uses the best of both worlds, ensuring a legacy of innovation and progress for generations to come.

When considering how to best utilize AI, I've developed a certain perspective that guides my decisions. Yes, AI is capable of handling complex tasks, but when it comes to the complicated, nuanced work that demands a human touch, I tend to rely on my team. AI's strength lies in its capacity for dealing with the heavy computational lifting, but for matters that require a deeper level of understanding, empathy, and discretion, human input remains indispensable.

Here's another of my guiding principles; allow the AI's strategic thought to be shaped by tactical tasks, not the other way around. As a leader, it's my responsibility to determine our strategy—where we invest our time and resources, the customers we target, the geographical markets we focus on, and whether our approach will be flexible and emergent or rigid and meticulously planned. It's my call to decide our priorities, our response to threats and opportunities, and how we allocate the resources at our disposal.

So, as much as I appreciate AI's potential, when it comes to strategy, that's my domain. I'll gladly let AI lend a helping hand by offloading a considerable chunk of the tactical work. By taking on more of the routine, complex tasks, AI can effectively free up more of my time and my team's energies, enabling us to focus on the critical strategic decisions that will define our path forward.

In this way, AI becomes a strategic partner of sorts, carrying out the tasks that it's best suited for, and giving us the space and time to handle those aspects where human insight and judgment are essential. We end up with a sort of symbiosis, where AI and humans each play to their strengths, leading to better outcomes all around.

With this book in your hands, you've got a super tool that can unlock your potential in the world of AI and business. But to really make this tool work magic, it's crucial to get a grip on the answers to the three big questions mentioned earlier.

Getting the hang of how AI works doesn't mean you have to be a whiz in coding or machine learning algorithms. It's more about having a basic understanding of what AI can and can't do, a kind of basic "AI know-how." It's about knowing enough to ask the right questions and make smart decisions.

When we're talking about what AI is really good at, we're talking about its power to really shake things up in areas like data analysis, automation, predictive modeling, and more. AI can, for example, breeze through a ton of data like nobody's business, spotting patterns and insights that a team of humans might take months or even years to figure out.

On the flip side, it's just as important to keep in mind the things we shouldn't trust AI to handle on its own. Despite being super smart and advanced, AI doesn't have the deep understanding, empathy, creativity, and good judgment that humans do. When it comes to tasks needing these human touchpoints, it's always a good call to keep AI as a helper, rather than handing over the reins completely.

With a clear idea of these three key questions, you're all set to use AI in a way that boosts your strengths, backs up your work, and most importantly, helps you build a better future for you and the world.

So, with this knowledge in your pocket, gear up for the challenge and get ready to shape an awesome future for you, your team, and the world. You can do this using AI as your sidekick, but remember to always let your human judgment and creativity lead the way in your decision making.

Go ahead and make your mark on the world.

About the Author

Amir Elkabir is a globally renowned expert in software delivery and applied AI. He has contributed to top tech magazines and frequently graces international stages as a speaker. Throughout his career, Amir has successfully led prominent AI and machine learning initiatives, now offering his expertise to leading organizations while holding executive roles in the industry.

An alumnus of MIT with an illustrious academic background, Amir has earned degrees from premier institutions, melding his deep knowledge in both technology and business. Currently, Amir calls multiple global cities his home and maintains a strong presence within the tech and business communities worldwide.

Index

OTHER TITLES IN THE COLLABORATIVE INTELLIGIENCE COLLECTION

Jim Spohrer and Haluk Demirkan, Editors

- *HR Tech Strategy* by Marlene de Koning
- *Let's Meet Blockchain* by Sylvain Metz
- *The Edge Data Center* by Hugh Taylor
- *Journey to the Metaverse* by Antonio Flores-Galea
- *Doing Digital* by Ved Sen
- *Breakthrough* by Martin Fleming
- *How Organizations Can Make the Most of Online Learning* by David Guralnick
- *Teaching Higher Education to Lead* by Sam Choon-Yin
- *Business and Emerging Technologies* by George Baffour
- *How to Talk to Data Scientists* by Jeremy Elser
- *Leadership in The Digital Age* by Niklas Hageback
- *Cultural Science* by William Sims Bainbridge

Concise and Applied Business Books

The Collection listed above is one of 30 business subject collections that Business Expert Press has grown to make BEP a premiere publisher of print and digital books. Our concise and applied books are for...

- Professionals and Practitioners
- Faculty who adopt our books for courses
- Librarians who know that BEP's Digital Libraries are a unique way to offer students ebooks to download, not restricted with any digital rights management
- Executive Training Course Leaders
- Business Seminar Organizers

Business Expert Press books are for anyone who needs to dig deeper on business ideas, goals, and solutions to everyday problems. Whether one print book, one ebook, or buying a digital library of 110 ebooks, we remain the affordable and smart way to be business smart. For more information, please visit www.businessexpertpress.com, or contact sales@businessexpertpress.com.

www.ingramcontent.com/pod-product-compliance
Lightning Source LLC
LaVergne TN
LVHW020807280325
806768LV00007B/55/J